D0882570

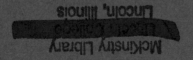

HONORARY
WHITE

HONORARY
WHITE

E.R. BRAITHWAITE

McGRAW-HILL BOOK COMPANY
New York   St. Louis   San Francisco
Düsseldorf   Mexico   Toronto

Design by Robert L. Mitchell.

Library of Congress Cataloging in Publication Data

Braithwaite, Edward Ricardo.
    Honorary white.

    Autobiographical.
    1. Africa, South—Race question.   2. Braithwaite, Edward Ricardo.   I.   Title.
DT763.B633   301.45′1′0968   74-30097
ISBN 0-07-007118-7

23456789BPBP798765

Books by
E. R. Braithwaite

TO SIR, WITH LOVE
A KIND OF HOMECOMING
PAID SERVANT
CHOICE OF STRAWS
RELUCTANT NEIGHBORS

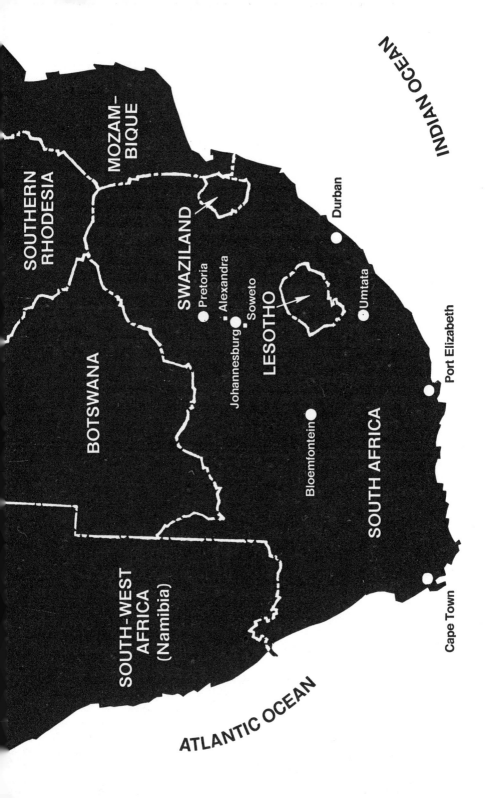

HONORARY
WHITE

1

My visit to South Africa really began the moment the huge Boeing 747 lifted off the tarmac at London's Heathrow airport and shuddered its way into the darkening sky. From that moment, my section of the lower rear cabin was transformed into a separate little world peopled by an impromptu, noisy mix of British, Americans, Swiss, Germans, South Africans, a few French, and me.

I sat watching and listening, especially to the emigrants. They were all British, suspended between the certainty of having finally discarded a familiar way of life and the uncertainties toward which they were being inexorably propelled. They were all young, aged between eighteen and thirty, and seemingly ill at ease as they recited the litany of troubles which had precipitated their decisions to leave Britain—the skyrocketing cost of living, restrictions on heating, lighting, and gasoline, the excessive cost of mortgages, strikes, competition with Blacks for jobs, and the inclement weather.

"We're doing it mainly for the children" was the excuse most frequently exchanged between them. I wondered why they found it necessary to make excuses for the decision to make a change, especially one so exciting and adventurous. The children, for their part, were soon running up and down the aisles and in and out of the toilets, happily unaware of the role they played in their parents' momentous decision.

At Nairobi, our first stop on African soil, some of the passengers departed and were replaced by British and South Africans linking up with us from other routes. All white. Not another black face in sight.

The other travelers had something else in common. They were all, in varying degrees, pleased and excited to be going or returning to South Africa. I was odd man out, wrapped in layers of uncertainty and apprehension, wondering whether and for how long I would be able to stay in an environment which would deliberately seek to humiliate and degrade me.

My fellow travelers knew the good life or anticipated a better one. Would any of them be able to understand my decision to expose myself voluntarily to a social order which would not only deny my humanity, but claim divine guidance and support for doing so? Ever since leaving the London airport, I had not exchanged a single word with anyone but the stewards, and then only in response to queries about meals. Was this a foretaste of what lay ahead?

Since boyhood in Guyana I had heard stories about horrors of life for Blacks in the gold, diamond, and coal mines of South Africa, and the cruel oppression they suffered at the hands of their European conquerors. I remember hearing about Blacks working deep in the bowels of the earth, day after day, ill-fed and poorly paid, completely at the mercy of the Whites who tyrannized and bullied them. Floods and cave-ins had trapped hundreds of these Blacks, and only token rescue efforts were made; their fate was of little consequence because they could so easily be replaced. We talked of these things, my boyhood friends and I, happily ignorant of the grimmer realities, safe in our freedom to move and speak, to see and learn, our discussions of the plight of our faraway black brethren hardly more than an academic exercise. In Guyana, the men who worked the gold, diamond, and bauxite deposits were called miners, but they all worked above ground, not like moles burrowing deep out of sight. The gold and diamond miners usually worked their own "claims," each hoping for the one big "strike" which would lift him overnight from penury to riches, meanwhile scratching a bare living from the reluctant earth. The bauxite miners worked for the Bauxite Company, balancing precariously between negotiations for better conditions and threats of a strike.

It was hard for my friends and me to take in the horror stories of long lines of ragged black men led docilely to and from the deep pits each day, under the cruelly watchful eyes of armed white guards. Why did they not turn on their oppressors the same way the Guyana sugar plantation workers sometimes did when the burden of long laborious hours with poor pay became unbearable? Blissfully young and arrogantly uninformed, we blamed the South African Blacks for being too timid and boasted among ourselves of what we would have done in similar circumstances.

As I grew up, it seemed that each successive South African Government instituted new and more oppressive laws against the black population, who seemed more and more resigned to their fate, or more and more helpless to change it. I met African Blacks for the first time during my student days in England. Though none of them was from South Africa they seemed well informed about life in the

Republic and excited my imagination with horror tales of white-settler inhumanity to the native Blacks. As they told it, the whole sorry business began with the establishment of a Dutch East India Company Trading Station at Table Bay and some mutinous personnel who later settled there as free farmers. Slaves from other parts of Africa were shipped there to help in the development of the settlement but were rigidly segregated, being denied even the right to wear shoes. As the settlement developed, the settlers or trekboers pushed into the interior, seizing the wide grazing grounds of the pastoral Hottentots, stealing their cattle, and killing the virtually defenseless Blacks.

"Those trekboers were all Calvinists and believed that God made the white man to rule over Blacks," one friend reminded me. "In fact they conceived of Blacks as being little more than animals. They would hold shooting competitions, with prizes going to the men who, in a stipulated time, killed the largest number of Blacks. Proof of a 'kill' was the severed penis of a male or two breasts of a female. Nothing new. The British did the same thing when they colonized Australia and Tasmania.

"Nothing has changed. Nothing," he said. "Sure, Blacks in South Africa wear shoes nowadays and are not arrested for smoking in the street. They're even allowed to work in offices or on building sites beside white men. But that means nothing. Whites still think the Blacks are animals. True, they're not shot for bounty like in the old days. Nowadays Blacks who step out of line are quickly arrested. The lucky ones are sent to jail; the others simply disappear."

"For what crime?" I asked. My friend evidently had a flair for dramatic overstatement.

"Crime? If you're black in South Africa that's the crime. Everything else is merely supporting evidence. To look a white man in the eye is a crime. To object when he abuses you is a crime. Everything you do is a crime. The State says so and the Church agrees."

When job-hunting in London in the summer of 1947, I met a black escapee from South Africa. At that time I was in the throes of despondency and disillusionment at the prejudice and discrimination I had encountered in Britain. It was in a coffee shop off Piccadilly Circus where I occasionally had a mug of hot tea and a thick cheese sandwich for my midday meal. Cheap and satisfying. He was there when I arrived and I deliberately took a seat near him. He smiled as I sat down.

"Hello, there," he greeted me, speaking with difficulty through a mouthful of fish and chips.

I was pleased at the prospect of a friendly interlude with another human being, particularly a black one. We'd understand each other.

"Where you from?" he wanted to know.

"Guyana."

"Been over here long?"

I mentioned that I'd come over eight years earlier and taken a degree at Cambridge and gone on to post-graduate studies. Then I had served in the R.A.F. Now I was job-hunting.

"You'll do all right," he assured me.

"Like hell I will. I've already been hunting nine months for a job. Any job."

"You've not been looking in the right places," he said. "I've been here two years and I've got a job. Got it six weeks after I arrived. Good job. No complaints." Smiling a white-toothed, superior, employed smile.

"Doing what?" I asked.

"Hospital orderly at Lewisham General."

"You like it there?"

"Sure. The pay's good. Lots of time off, and the work's not hard. You should try it."

"No thanks." The idea of working in a sterile hospital ward ministering to ailing, irritable people did not appeal to me.

"Then what are you complaining about? You want a job, don't you?"

"I'm looking for a job I'm qualified to do."

"Man, you're lucky you can pick and choose. Where I come from you take what they give you."

"Where's that?"

"Cape Town. South Africa. I finished high school, but the only job I could get was messenger boy in a grocery store. Sweep out the store and carry groceries for the Whites. One Rand a week."

"How much is that in English money?"

"About eighteen shillings."

"So you decided to come over here," I said.

"You make it sound so easy, man. As if I walked up to the steamship office and said 'I'm going to England, here's the money for my fare.' Hell, I walked to Port Elizabeth, then stowed away on a British ship for Southampton."

"Just like that?"

"Oh, they found me when we were halfway across. Made me wash decks and help in the galley. But here I am."

"And here you stay," I added.

"Hell, yes. I'd rather die than go back. In South Africa a black man is treated like an animal. Your degrees wouldn't be worth a damn. Anyway, you couldn't get into the universities, not the white ones."

In 1960 I received an appointment as Human Rights Officer for the World Veterans Federation at the Federation's headquarters in Paris and met many South Africans who lived there, most of them painters, writers, or musicians. They all saw themselves as voluntary refugees from a repressive police state. Sometimes over coffee at an outdoor Left Bank restaurant I'd join in lively discussion with them and a few expatriate Americans, black and white. I learned that, even with lynch law at its worst, life in the southern United States was far better for Blacks than in South Africa. At that time Blacks in the American South had limited voting rights while Blacks in South Africa were not even included in the national census, because they were not considered human. In the United States Blacks could seek redress for injustice in the Federal courts, either directly or through legal representation; in South Africa the courts themselves enforced discriminatory practices. Apart from me, all those who took part in the conversations had first-hand experience of the oppression they described, and the picture they drew of the life of Blacks in South Africa was frightening—a society where the owner of a black skin was helplessly subjected to exploitation, ill-treatment, and the death penalty.

Early in 1965 I was appointed Guyana's Ambassador to the United Nations and met more South Africans in New York, white and black. Some of the Whites, churchmen and others of liberal persuasion, were petitioners against the racist regime; but the majority were businessmen, employees of the South African Government, and tourists. Always acutely aware of the overwhelming antipathy to their Government, they were continually on the defensive, insisting that outsiders could not appreciate the peculiar conditions of South Africa. Without exception, the South African Blacks I met were petitioners, escapees, and permanent exiles from their country, and committed to persuading United Nations member states to deny any aid or support to South Africa.

In 1966 the United Nations General Assembly voted overwhelmingly to terminate South Africa's mandate to supervise and control South West Africa, now Namibia, and itself assumed full responsibility for the territory. I was very active in the special committee which designed the resolution and lobbied for its passage until finally the United Nations Council for South West Africa was set up. I was made President of that Council.

I plunged enthusiastically into the struggle to free Namibia from the defacto control of South Africa. But although I then became directly involved with the fate of the Blacks of Southern Africa, my prime interest at the time lay in showing that I was fully professional, so as to demonstrate that representatives from the smallest, least powerful, and poorest of member nations could effectively conduct the business of the United Nations.

Some of the black petitioners were impatient with the careful way in which I approached their complaints. They clearly expected of me a more immediate identification with their situation and were not the least bit impressed by my posture of scrupulous impartiality. During a session with a group of exiles from Namibia one of them impatiently asked,

"Mr. Ambassador, whose side are you on?"

Many a petitioner would say "You ought to go and see for yourself," as I failed to comprehend the horrors they tried to convey: police brutality; arrest and imprisonment without legal defense; trials which mocked justice; Blacks routinely sentenced to banishment and death; Blacks barred by law from voting; Blacks forbidden to organize labor unions, banned from all but the lowest work categories. It was all new to me. The British who had governed Guyana were no strangers to prejudice and discrimination, but nothing in their treatment of that predominantly black population in any way compared with the terrible stories I heard from the South African petitioners. It was not painful for me to reflect on British Guiana's civil service, schools, colleges, police, communications, utilities, and courts—all managed and operated by Blacks under white supervision which was more ritual than functional. Then, as now, the busiest places in the country were the courts, forever crowded with litigants and their representatives, as if everyone was determined to prove his access to equal justice.

The Government of South Africa pointedly ignored the new Council. Several requests for permission to visit Namibia were either unanswered or peremptorily refused. On one occasion, I made a personal appeal for a meeting of the U.N. Security Council on behalf of a group of Namibian Blacks who had been abducted within their country by South African Security Police and taken to South Africa where they were charged with treason, tried, and pronounced guilty. The members of the Security Council individually expressed their distaste for South Africa's action and, in carefully guarded language, condemned her intrusion into the territory over which she no longer had legal control. However, no resolution emerged from the meeting, nor was there any collective statement of condemnation of South Africa. The Blacks were hanged.

"Go and see for yourself," the petitioners urged, though they knew that the Council and I would not be permitted to enter South Africa or Namibia. And while I sometimes heard myself echoing the same refrain, I knew that I would not willingly have exposed myself to life in South Africa. So I played with the thought of going there, secure in the knowledge that I would not be allowed in. But the thought often haunted me: Just suppose the South African Government suddenly relented?

Just supposing one day there came a letter of clearance for the Council to visit Namibia? My colleagues and I, black and white, would have to go through South Africa. Would we be allowed to travel together, eat together, use the same hotel? Or would we be segregated according to South Africa's racial policies? Would I accept such segregation as secondary to the main issue of fact-finding? Perhaps, as a native of another sovereign country and under the protection of the United Nations I would not be subject to South Africa's segregation laws. But, if insulated from them, how could I truly appreciate their effect?

It would be a harsh irony for me, a black man, to visit a country like Namibia or South Africa and be isolated from the cruelties to which other black men were continually subjected. How would the Blacks themselves react to me, a "protected" person? Would they respond to me as a black "brother" or merely as a representative of the United Nations who happened to be black but was unlikely to be concerned for their plight? I was not an African, had no knowledge of their languages and no real understanding of their traditions, so I would be as much an outsider as anyone else.

Early in 1973, long after I had left the U.N., a friend in Guyana sent me a clipping from the South African *Official Gazette*. The clipping stated that, as of that date, the ban on all books by E. R. Braithwaite was lifted. I was surprised and, on impulse, telephoned the South African Consul General in New York. I said that I had just learned of the lifting of the ban from my books, and even as I thought of it, asked whether the ban was lifted from the author as well.

The Consul General was friendly and charming and completely and happily unaware of author, books, or ban. We chatted awhile and he suggested that the best way of checking any ban on myself was by applying for a visa. All visa applications are processed in Pretoria and a successful application would mean there was no ban. He invited me to visit his office at my convenience and make the application.

He was as friendly, courteous and urbane as his voice had promised. With the utmost civility we talked about his country and its policies and he said that he sincerely hoped my visa application would be favorably considered and that I might at close quarters come to an appreciation of why such policies and practices were necessary in the prevailing circumstances. I told him that everything I had heard about his country had already prejudiced me against that likelihood.

"Be patient. Go and see for yourself," he said, unwittingly echoing the others. He sounded as if he expected the visa to be granted. Would he, as Consul General, advise that I be given one? I suddenly felt cornered. Supposing, just supposing the visa was granted. What then? I was not attracted to the idea of spending any time in a racist society. So why bother to apply for a visa? If it was granted and I refused it, that would be the end of me as a critic of South Africa.

But there seemed little chance that the visa would actually be granted. Surely it would suffer the same fate as those earlier Council appeals. So security-conscious a state as South Africa would certainly investigate my background, especially my anti–South Africa position at the United Nations. Their conclusions would certainly be neg-

ative. In any case, I could tell myself that I had tried to visit
South Africa. I'd be able to put the "Go see for yourself"
thing to rest once and for all.

Five months passed with no word from Pretoria and I
had convinced myself that my application had been
ignored, when there was a telephone call from the Consul
General. My visa had been granted. My immediate reaction
was one of acute distress. Now that my way was clear, the
thought of actually going to South Africa was abhorrent.
For his part, the Consul General believed I sincerely
wished to visit his country and invited me to come to the
Consulate again and meet other members of his staff who
would provide me with a useful overview. I accepted.

They seemed to be calling my bluff. For years now I
had been so safe in my posture of justified condemnation of
South Africa's racial policies, isolated from whatever the
grim realities might be. Everyone knew that South Africa
was closed to critical inspection, especially by Blacks, so I
was safe in my hawk's nest. Until now. What would I say
to the Consul General? What excuse could I fabricate to
explain my rejection of the visa?

But, on the other hand, why reject it? So far, I had
given full credence to South Africa's critics and had readily
allied myself with them. Well, why not see for myself, as so
many of them had advised? No matter how trying the
circumstances, I had the right, as a visitor, to leave whenever I chose. Yet, at my age, and accustomed to freedom of
movement, speech and association, could I tolerate even for
a short time the contempt, restriction, and discourtesy
which were inescapable if I entered South Africa?

Would I be willing to obey the "Whites Only" signs,
ignore the "kaffir" epithet, and give way to Whites? I
doubted that I could. Yet how could I ever meet and talk
with South African Blacks on their own earth except by

going there? Out of the blue was handed me the opportunity to "see for myself." Didn't I have a duty to seize it? Should I reject it on the flimsy excuse of safety or sensitivity to anti-Black attitudes? My doubts and dread nagged me like a toothache, but I knew I was going to go.

The stewardess announced that we were making our descent to Johannesburg and I began mentally preparing myself for what I felt sure would be my first test. What would I do when confronted with the "Whites Only" signs? Would I have to undergo a separate passport and customs check? Would the humiliations I had heard about begin then or later?

Preoccupied with these speculations, I hardly noticed that the huge plane had landed, was taxiing to its gate. There followed the gathering up of personal belongings and the long line through the narrow exit to the shock of warm sunshine on the short walk to the cavernous customs hall.

Try as I might, the only signs I could locate were those over the narrow gateways to the passport control desks distinguishing between South African nationals and others. In my turn I was shown the same courteous treatment as anyone else and moved into the baggage claim area where I grabbed a metal pushcart just ahead of someone else. With nothing to declare I pushed my bags through customs and outside into whatever the next several weeks would disclose.

2

My hotel was a new one on the edge of the business district, pompously dominating a busy crossroads and overlooking a block-square park, a green oasis amid the steel, glass, and concrete. My car had barely stopped when the door was yanked open by a Black, the doorman—tall, muscular, and resplendent in gray top hat, matching pearl gray tail suit, black tie, and gleaming black shoes. He helped me out of the car, smiled broadly, and greeted me in what sounded like Afrikaans but changed quickly to English when he noticed my failure to respond. He seemed surprised that only I, and not my white driver as well, would be staying at the hotel.

Inside, the hotel was even more imposing. The lobby was spacious, with leather divans spotted like islands on a placid sea. Artfully carved and paneled woodwork on the walls highlighted a wide wooden staircase leading upward to the mezzanine floor. The doorman led me to the reception desk and presented me with something of a flourish. The white reception staff were all aplomb and courtesy as if well prepared for my coming. Gray-suited porters everywhere. "Good morning, sir." One of them introduced himself to me as the manager. "I trust you had a comfortable flight." I thanked him and said I had. "We are very happy to have you staying with us," he went on, motioning me to a table to which he brought a pen and registration cards and showed me where he needed my signature. My name and flight particulars had already been entered on the card, which surprised me until I remembered that in New York I had been advised to make my travel plans through the Grosvenor Tours Company and they had chosen this hotel for me.

The formalities completed, I was shown to my suite, large and comfortably cool. Two porters followed with my luggage. They were black, gray suited, and, I noticed, were scrutinizing me carefully. When the manager left, one of the porters addressed me in what I presumed was an African dialect.

"I don't understand," I told him.

"You're not African?" he asked, in English.

"No."

"Where are you from?" meanwhile busying themselves with my luggage.

"Guyana." The look on their faces told me the name meant nothing to them.

"Where's that?"

"South America."

"America. That where Mr. Bob Foster is from. Do you know Mr. Bob Foster, sir."

"No. Who is he?"

"A boxing champion." Proudly. "He stayed here in this hotel." Looking at me as if that bit of information was important and should be received respectfully. I nodded, accepting.

"You a boxer?" he asked.

"No. I write books."

He left me with the feeling that as a non-boxer, I held no further interest for him. Later I learned that Bob Foster, the boxer, had not only stayed here but had been the guest of honor, cutting the ribbon which officially opened the hotel for public business. I also learned that it was no accident which brought me here.

According to South African law, a hotel can accept non-white guests only if it obtains a special permit or license to do so, and very few such permits are issued. Non-Whites are Blacks, Asians, and those of mixed blood (Coloreds). Ironically, only the best, the five-star hotels, are licensed to accommodate Non-Whites. Native Non-Whites, of course, rarely have either the means or the temerity to use these hotels. To complicate the situation further, visiting Non-Whites are designated "Honorary White" to insure, it is claimed, their insulation and exemption from the many embarrassments which would otherwise attend them. I discovered that this title was first conceived to meet the special circumstances of Japanese businessmen who came to establish footholds for their companies in the South African market. They could not, like indigenous Non-Whites, be contemptuously restricted and segregated, so it was decided to "whiten" them for as long as they lived and worked in South Africa. Eventually, all non-white visitors were called "Honorary White."

Outside, it was sunny and uncomfortably hot; inside it was refreshingly cool from air conditioning and the fine mesh curtains drawn across the large windows which overlooked the street. I prowled around to familiarize myself with what would be my point of departure for the next six weeks. The vestibule was equipped with a washroom and cloak room for visitors and led into the spacious, attractive dining area. This contained a large wooden table, polished to a dazzling shine, and six matching chairs. The nearby wall was really a cupboard artfully contrived to hide a small refrigerator and shelves for pots and pans, cutlery and glassware. A room divider of simulated bamboo partly separated this from the lounge, large and luxurious and painfully overdone in green—olive green carpet, paler green walls, a glass-topped center table which held a large basket of fruit, lime green upholstered furniture, pictures in contrasting shades of green, and, scattered about the room, an abundance of artificial plants.

Luckily, the bedroom door could be closed to shut out the green menace from the more somber but equally lush comfort of the large, canopied bed in polished dark wood, matching side tables, highboy, and chest of drawers. Near the window was a wide writing table and two chairs with elephant hide seats. One entire wall seemed to glide away at a touch to reveal ample closet space for clothing and luggage.

The bathroom was nearly as large as the bedroom and completely lined in glistening brown tile. Twin washbowls and mirrors, a large deep bath, bidet, separate shower stall, a telephone, and piped music. Many towels were piled beside the washbowls and hung from racks near the bath and shower stall. The radio and piped music could be controlled from several points throughout the suite.

So this was the five-star treatment. It was not what I would have chosen if the choice had been mine. Whites could choose according to the dictates of their pocketbooks; visiting Blacks must pay the top price.

I dialed room service for a cold drink. The young, black attendant seemed very surprised yet pleased to discover that I was black, and said something to me in a language I could not understand.

"I'm afraid I don't speak your language," I replied.

"You're not Zulu?" he asked.

"No." I was secretly flattered at his mistake.

"Where you from?" he wanted to know.

"South America," I said.

"You know Mr. Bob Foster, sir?"

"No."

"He's from your country."

"No. He's from the United States." Realizing, from his expression, that the small geographical difference did not impress him.

"He lived in this hotel," he said. Then, smiling, "He's a great boxer. A big champion. He beat the white man. He beat the South African." The smile was wide. I paid and he left. Evidently, Mr. Bob Foster had made a deep impression here.

Sipping my drink, I opened the curtains and looked out onto the small park which occupied the block directly opposite. It contained neatly trimmed lawns, flowering shrubs, a central fountain of concrete slabs arranged to simulate a miniature waterfall, and shade trees casually spaced around its perimeter. A tiled walkway neatly bisected this handsome park, and an iron fence enclosed it on all sides, broken only by the wide gates at each end of the walkway. Benches were scattered under the trees, and these were all occupied by young black men and women chatting together or merely dozing in the sun. Sprawled on the grass near one flowering bush were three men, two of them white and all of them unkempt, who lazily passed a bottle from one to another. Here and there were forms face down on the lawn, seemingly asleep. White men and women hurried through the park, intent on whatever their business might be; the unemployed sat in the sun, in their idleness and, perhaps, in their dreams.

I took the lift downstairs and crossed the street into the park. This was as good a place to begin as any; I might as well plunge in. I walked across the lawn to a group sitting under a tree. Two men and a woman, all black, watched my approach in silence.

"Good afternoon," I greeted them. No sign of welcome on any face. Then one of the men responded with a slight nod and a barely audible growl. Not to be put off, I persisted.

"I'm a stranger visiting your country." This seemed to stir some small interest. Press on, I told myself.

"If I wasn't sure that I'd made a long trip to be here, I could easily imagine this was England. Same lawns, same trees, and same green benches." I waited to see some faint hint of interest.

"You from England?" the woman asked, making it sound like an accusation, not believing it.

"I took the plane in London," I replied. "Actually, I now live in the United States, but I once lived in London for many years."

"Yes, but where are you from?" the woman persisted.

"South America. Guyana. That's where I was born."

"Bob Foster is from America," one man said, smiling not at me, but to the happy memory of whatever images the name Foster conjured up for him. "You know him?"

"No," I said. "How are things with you?" I felt somewhat intrusive but needed to establish some basis for conversation. They exchanged glances and one of the men, bald and sparsely bearded, said something in what I guessed was an African language or dialect. Not knowing what he'd said, I said nothing.

"You from Lesotho?" the bald one asked. That surprised me because I'd already told him where I came from and I was sure he'd heard enough to know that I was not indigenous African. Maybe they were playing a little game with me.

"No. I'm from America." North or south was not really important at this point. The woman said something quite unintelligible, and the bald one said, "No work," spreading his long-fingered hands in a wide gesture to include his companions. They were all neatly dressed, the men in dark suits, white open-necked shirts, and shoes thinly filmed with red dust as if they had done much walking. The woman, young, round-faced, and sturdily built, wore a simple cotton frock in a bright print, her stockingless feet brown and shapely in white sandals.

"You working?" she asked.

"Yes."

"But now? Here?"

"Here I'm on holiday. Just visiting," I replied. "Do you live nearby?" They looked at each other and laughed in that sharp humorless way which is both bitter and contemptuous, as if I had committed some small stupidity.

"Live nearby?" they mimicked. "No, we live in Soweto." Then, waving an arm to include the whole park, the bald man added, "We all live in Soweto. We come in each morning looking for work and we go back each night. We don't live here."

Abruptly he turned away and talked rapidly with his companions, their unfamiliar language shutting me out completely.

They seemed to have no further interest in me, offering no response when I said goodbye and left them to wander around the park and out into the bustling streets amid the noise of traffic and construction.

Along the narrow pavements, Whites hurrying to and

fro, purposefully. Blacks moving with the stream, many of them in the uniforms of servitude—messengers, maids, porters; on their faces the patient dignity etched deeply by centuries of survival. I wondered what went on behind these smooth black masks of people forced by law into the most menial of work and always under the watchful eye of police who were everywhere in view: large powerful men red-faced from the heat, projecting a certain surly contempt for everyone in general and Blacks in particular. Jackbooted, helmeted, and sometimes armed, they seemed handpicked for the role of controlling others through fear.

I returned to my hotel to make some telephone calls, contacts with friends of friends, people who might be able to tell me about various aspects of life in South Africa, and was deeply encouraged by their friendliness.

I switched on the radio in my bedroom. After a few moments of music, a program was announced entitled "Annie, Get Your Gun." I was about to change the station, thinking it was the old musical production, when the announcer explained that it was that week's installment of a program on guns for housewives. Fascinated, I listened to the advice on the purchase, handling, and maintenance of firearms and ammunition of various types.

The implication was inescapable. The enemy against whom the radio audience was warned, the "they" against whom Annie was being taught to point her gun, aim, and slowly squeeze the trigger was the Blacks, the same who cooked Annie's meals, cared for her children, cleaned her house, washed and ironed her clothes, trimmed her lawns, ran errands for her husband and provided the basic foundation from which she enjoyed a comfortable living with enough left over for guns and bullets.

That evening I made my first social call in South

Africa on Helen Suzman, to whom I had been introduced through letters by a mutual friend in New York. A Progressive Party member of the South African Parliament, Helen Suzman was internationally known as an outspoken critic of apartheid. She had invited me to dine with her family and a small group of personal friends. At her suggestion, I arrived early to give us an opportunity to talk before the other guests arrived.

She met me at the door and led me through the house to a rear patio which overlooked a spacious tree-shaded lawn.

"I'm baby-sitting, so I hope you don't mind if we sit out here. I can keep an eye on my grandchildren," she said, pointing to two small, chubby children playing in a corner of the lawn. Tall and suntanned, she moved with an easy grace, as if completely confident of herself.

"My son and his wife are visiting from England, and one of my daughters is home from the United States. Those two are my son's children. Wonderful to have them around. Keeps me young," she said, smiling. "I'm Helen. What do I call you?"

"Ted."

"Well, Ted, welcome to South Africa, and I hope you see and hear enough to make the trip worthwhile."

"Thank you."

"I know a little about you. When Lillian Poses wrote me that you were coming I checked you out. Your books, I mean. From the library. The film of *To Sir, with Love* was very popular here. Especially the private showings, you know, the uncut version."

"Can't think what anyone could find necessary to cut in that film," I said.

"This is South Africa, my friend," she said. "Can't

publicize the idea of a black and a white teacher getting too chummy. Especially if one of them is a woman. Worse yet, teenage, white, girl students having a crush on a black teacher! Tut, tut." The smile breaking through to undermine the mock severity of her tone.

"Couldn't have been much left of the film if they cut all that out," I suggested.

"I wouldn't know, as I didn't see the cut version. But I do know it was very popular.' People crying buckets into their hankies. It was banned for a while, you know."

"Yes, I heard. I even met one of the MPs who sat on the committee which imposed the ban. A Mr. Englebrecht. But that same committee later rescinded the ban and Englebrecht admitted that he and his family enjoyed the film."

"That's part of our problem, going around in circles where Blacks are concerned. On the one hand we promote the myth of the inferior Black while on the other we refuse to look at him for fear of discovering his equal humanity. I hear that you plan to spend some time in South Africa. How long?"

"As long as I can bear it," I replied.

"Oh, you look fit enough," she laughed.

"I was thinking of my spirit," I said.

"So was I. How do you plan to move about and where do you intend to go?"

"I've arranged for a car and driver for trips outside Johannesburg. In the city, I intend to use whatever public transport is available. I'd like to visit as much of the country as possible, particularly the Bantustans."

"The new name for them is 'Homelands,'" she smiled, as if the name conjured up for her some particular irony. "One word of advice. This is not London or New York. You can't get on any bus or hail any taxi you see. If you have a car at your disposal, use it. Understand?"

"Understand."

"No point in exposing yourself to unnecessary embarrassment." She excused herself to step into the garden and adjudicate a minor argument between the children, returning within a few minutes. Her movements were quick and controlled.

"That's part of my dilemma," I continued when she returned. "I want to avoid embarrassment to myself, but I also want to have a clear idea of what life is like for a Black in this society. I'm sure I'll learn nothing if I'm preoccupied with my own comfort and sensitivity."

"Being insulted and abused won't help either. If you want to know what it's like for Blacks in this society, talk to them. Ask them. They might not tell you, but ask them just the same."

"Why wouldn't they tell me?"

"They might not trust you."

"I'll take that chance. Could you introduce me to some of them?"

"I don't know that that will help you. Some of them talk with me, but I'm not sure that they trust me. Don't blame them. In their position I might not trust me either."

"In New York, I was told that you are perhaps the only White in Parliament who speaks on behalf of Blacks."

"You were told wrong. I speak up against repressive governmental policies. I speak against the arbitrary way in which those policies are imposed on our citizens, black and white. I speak against house arrest, banning and jail sentences for those who criticize the Government. I speak against disenfranchisement of all Blacks. Actually, I think it would be truer to say that I speak against the inequities in our society rather than for any particular group."

"But I heard that Blacks are more favorably disposed to you than to other Whites."

"You're very kind." Again that quick, lively smile. "Although, come the crunch, I don't know that that would save me. Anyway, I don't think I can be much help with introductions. At this time, most politicians are busy in their constituencies getting themselves ready for the opening of Parliament next week in Cape Town."

"I plan to visit Cape Town. Mr. Englebrecht promised to arrange meetings with the Foreign Minister, the Minister for Bantu Affairs, and, if possible, the Prime Minister."

"Fine, then you'll be well taken care of. Anyway, phone me when you're there and we'll have lunch together or something."

We were joined by Helen's daughter, son and daughter-in-law, and Helen's husband. The children ran in from their play to be fussed over and conversation became general. I learned that the son and daughter were both living and practicing their separate professions overseas because they preferred the freer societies of Britain and the United States. Dr. Suzman, a slight, graying man, said little, yet there was an aura of strength about him. Perhaps he supplied the anchorage which secured and sustained Helen.

In time, the other guests arrived and we were introduced. Most of them were Afrikaners, members of the dominant white group, supporters of the Nationalists, the political party in power. I had no idea whether Helen had told them much or anything about me to prepare them for the encounter, but I immediately sensed their effort to appear cosmopolitan, able to consort easily with anyone. The handshakes pumped a bit too hard, the greetings a shade too hearty. The few other guests were British, that is, they were of British rather than Boer extraction and proudly English-speaking. I'd heard that there existed a wide philosophical gulf between these people, their common whiteness notwithstanding. Perhaps there is a real difference, but apart from the somewhat heavily accented English of the Afrikaners, to which my ear quickly became attuned, they appeared the same to me. White.

"Tell me, Mr. Braithwaite," I was asked, "what's your impression of our country?" A stocky, florid man in, I guessed, his early fifties, well-groomed, well-rounded, exuding an air of substance. He had been introduced as a banker, and looked the part, although his grip as we shook hands was strong and forceful and suggested he spent as much time outdoors using his muscles as indoors using his banking skills. His round, pleasant face seemed accustomed to smiling easily as if his course through life avoided the rocks and shoals which battered the less fortunate.

"I've been here only a day," I replied, "hardly enough time to form an impression."

"But surely you have some feel of the place," he countered, smiling. "You writers are supposed to possess a special sensitivity to atmosphere. You have the advantage of viewing things with both an inner and outer eye, which suggests that you see more and in a shorter time than the rest of us."

I wasn't sure about him. The bonhomie came so easily. All I'd heard about South Africans in general and Afrikaners in particular had warned me to be wary of them. Was this one being complimentary or mocking? I thought I'd play it safe.

"I don't consider myself specially equipped to view you or anyone else, so I prefer to take time in looking." The rest of them were looking and listening to us.

"May I ask the same question, but in another way?" another guest interposed. Voice, casual manner, all of a piece, proclaiming the Britisher. Perhaps deliberately so to emphasize some difference from the Afrikaners. This gentleman was tall, lanky in his baggy but well-cut clothes. Thin-faced and sad-eyed. I wondered whether he was an immigrant or a native. So difficult to tell with the British. They can remain considerably aloof from a community even if they were born in it, as if geographical locations were merely accidents of fortune with no formative influence on their ancestral character. He went on.

"Did you have some personal view of South Africa in advance of your decision to visit us?" Even if he wasn't a native, he certainly seemed to feel at home. "Us," he'd said.

"Certainly."

"Would you like to tell us about it?"

"Why not?" I decided to lay it on their collective plate and watch the reaction.

"Simply stated, it was a negative view. Some of it derived from those white South Africans, officials and others, who tried to defend your policies and were obviously uncomfortable about it; some of it from other white South Africans, mainly churchmen, whose conscience made them resist those policies and who suffered house arrest, banning, and sometimes imprisonment. But most of it came from Blacks of both South Africa and Namibia who were victimized by those policies and were lucky enough to escape. I found their stories most persuasive."

"And would you, as a writer, be content with that?"

"Surely my presence here is answer enough. However, while at the United Nations I noticed that even those countries which seemed most friendly to South Africa never publicly defended her policies. Still, I am here and will try to be as objective as the situation will let me."

Hell, I didn't need to sugarcoat anything for them.

"Perhaps, while you're here, we can change your

view," the banker said. "Providing you are willing to subdue your prejudices. Many people from outside our country are deeply prejudiced against us without knowing anything about how we came to be what we are, how we function as a people, and the real nature of the relationship between us and the Bantu nation."

"Nation?" I asked. "I thought that, Black and White, you were all one nation."

"That's a common misconception." He smiled, assured that he spoke for all of them. "The Blacks are a separate people, several nations, in fact. Language, customs, religions. They're not the collective group outsiders imagine them to be. I know. I grew up with them and speak several of their languages. Among themselves they are as different from each other as they are from us. Our policy, simply stated, is to respect those differences, and as circumstances dictate, preserve them."

"Have you decided all this for them or with them?"

"Come now, let's be quite frank with each other," he admonished, still smiling. "Our predecessors fought and conquered the Bantu and, like conquered people everywhere, they became subject people. Subject people are never treated as equals, at least not until prevailing political and economic conditions dictate such a step. The Bantu outnumber us ten to one, at least, and we cannot now or in the foreseeable future allow them any conditions or circumstances which could precipitate armed conflict with us. We must protect ourselves against them. Outsiders don't understand this. Actually, we live in fear of them."

"You, in fear of them? In the few hours I've been here, I would guess that the shoe is on the other foot," I said.

"He's right, but for all the wrong reasons," said Helen's daughter. Her dark eyes flashed under a short crop of brown hair, everything about her explosively vital, in marked contrast to her calm, unflappable mother. "Of course we're afraid, but we deliberately create and maintain the awful conditions under which the Blacks live, then we watch them for signs of revolt. If there's no sign, we pressure them a little more. So it goes on. We're afraid of their numbers, but, in our fear we seem to want to woo the very danger which threatens us. It's a vicious cycle. I couldn't function in such an atmosphere, so I cleared off."

"We can't all exercise such a happy choice," the Englishman said. "Some of us must accept the responsibility for finding a formula which would allow—"

"What formula?" I interrupted. "For more than a century, the Blacks have been completely disarmed, tribally dislocated, disenfranchised, and displaced. Given your economic power, your command of military personnel and weapons, the fear of them which you express seems to me at best dubious."

"It's not as easy as that," the banker interposed. "I'm sure you appreciate that even the most sophisticated arms in the hands of a few cannot always resist the resolute pressure of an unarmed or primitively armed mob." The smile was there, as if he already rejected the image his words conjured up. "However, we hope it will never come to such a bloody test. In spite of what you have certainly heard to the contrary, we are not completely against change. We welcome change, providing it is orderly. We welcome evolution, with everyone developing in his own way, at his own pace, with his own kind. It is revolution that we oppose."

Several others intervened now, as if triggered by the word revolution. One elderly gray-haired couple kept determinedly out of it. From the few words they spoke, I guessed that they were Afrikaners. They seemed ill at ease and I wondered why they were there. Maybe Helen had her reasons. Maybe they simply weren't used to meeting Blacks, even one unarmed Black from overseas.

"How can you claim to favor the development of the Blacks in their own way, at their own pace and with their own kind if you reserve to yourself the right to control that way and that pace?"

"For the time being, my friend," the banker insisted, "only for the time being. Our Bantu people are not like you, educated and sophisticated . . ."

"I met some in New York, petitioners against your policies. They seemed sophisticated enough for me to believe them highly educated," I told him. "Some of them are products of your university system."

"Any glib dissident could sound off at the United Nations," returned the banker, with a trace of heat. "Anyone who is against South Africa is sure of a hearing there. Our Bantu people need to be educated into the responsibilities of government. We have designed an educational system which will provide them with the necessary skills."

"Wouldn't they have acquired those skills in your established universities?"

"We do not wish the black man to be a carbon copy of ourselves. Anyway, it is easy to see you have been told a great deal about us, all of it to our disadvantage." They were all watching me, Helen aloof from it as if she had provided the stage for this encounter and was letting it take its course.

"I told you so earlier this evening," I reminded him. "It seems to me that if your claims of goodwill are genuine, you should be having this kind of dialogue with South African Blacks. Do you? I'll be here today and gone tomorrow. Why not give them an opportunity of testing your goodwill?"

"It's not easy," someone else interrupted. "Few of us know the Bantu except as employees, and fewer of us want to know him in any other relationship."

"That's only half of it," from another. "Overtures of friendship from us are likely to be met with hostility and suspicion."

"Only a moment ago, you claimed the right to determine the pace and scope of their destiny, now you say you don't know them," I said. "Anyway, shouldn't you take a risk with them, just as you did with me?"

"It was no risk at all," the Englishman intervened. "We know your books and they gave us a rather good idea of who you are."

"That may be," I retorted, not wishing to let him off, "but I am no less opposed to your policies than is any local black man you can think of. I hope my books made that clear."

"Perhaps, perhaps," replied the banker, "but for the moment you are here with us, so let's talk with you. You represent the world view of us, and we are not insensitive to that view. What many outsiders do not know is that, in our own way, we are striving to redress some of the inequities in our society. Compared to what is happening in some other places, you might notice nothing or very little, but change is occurring nonetheless. In sport, for example."

"Are you referring to the fact that a black American fought your white champion here recently? And defeated him?" I deliberately added the last bit for good measure, trying to put a small dent in the armor of their secure rightness. He ignored it.

"That, and other things. Arthur Ashe was here competing in our tennis tournament. Insignificant it may seem to you, but for us it is an important beginning. Let me tell you of another advance. I have for years been a member of an exclusive club here in Johannesburg whose members were only Afrikaner Whites. English-speaking Whites were not admitted. Not long ago, on my initiative, an English-speaking person was elected, so, quietly but effectively, the old order has changed."

"The next move should be to offer membership to a Black." This was deliberate provocation, but nobody bit.

"No, the next move is to invite you to come and meet us. Come and talk with the members of my club, all of us dyed-in-the-wool, intransigent conservative Boers, as you see us. Come and do us the courtesy of hearing our point of view. Doesn't mean you have to agree with it, but at least hear us."

The others seemed as surprised as I was by his invitation. Shocked even. I watched the man, his eyes mischievously glistening in the smooth, smiling face. Was he playing with me, knowing I would refuse his offer? Was this a way of finally stifling my criticism? No doubt I'd been coming on a bit strong.

"I can't imagine that any useful purpose could be served by my visiting your club," I temporized.

"How do you know?" he replied. "What's your private formula for change? How do you decide what might precipitate some small change, or even some big change? Come and talk with us. I promise you we will listen courteously to your criticism of us and I hope you in turn will hear us out."

"Why don't you?" Helen urged me.

The elderly, graying couple were frowning, as if they were not very happy with this turn of events.

"Perhaps our visitor prefers to condemn from the outside," the Englishman offered. "It's simpler that way."

"That's not my concern," I said to him, to all of them. "I'm asking myself why I should be the one when it would be even easier for you to invite a local Black. From what I've already heard, they speak both English and Afrikaans. If some challenge is intended, wouldn't it be better directed to one of them?"

"Ah, a challenge is intended," the banker seized on it. "You are here, you have been critical of us and I'm saying to you, 'Come and meet us in one of our strongholds.' Yes, it is a challenge, Mr. Braithwaite. From outside, you castigate us without really knowing anything about us. Now, in fact, I'm going out on a limb by inviting you, a black man, to come and justify the invitation to my brother members. You might not think so, but this in itself is a giant step."

A friend in New York, on hearing of my intention to visit South Africa, had warned that the granting of a visa to me was no innocent act; it meant that there was a plan to use me somehow to South Africa's advantage. Now I asked myself, was this part of the plan? Had I been deliberately inveigled into something? I couldn't believe that. The invitation, challenge, had emerged far too naturally, and besides, Helen would never lend herself to that kind of sleazy plotting. I must be careful to avoid reading evil intent into everything.

The challenge was more like a dare, and he seemed to be daring himself rather than me. Daring himself to carry off another first? An Englishman, and now a Black? Perhaps I did him an injustice, perhaps he was completely sincere in all he said. But how would I feel meeting with a group of men psychologically, philosophically, and spiritually conditioned to see Blacks, myself included, as barely human and undeserving of ordinary human treatment?

"Well?" he prodded. They all seemed to be waiting for my answer. I wondered if I was making far too much of the situation. In my work and travel in the United States, I'd eaten and talked with men who, upon examination, were no less bigoted than South Africans are reputed to be. If this man, himself a product of the environment and conditioning which nurtured the hates and fears within this society, was willing to make a gesture, should I reject it? Call it dare or challenge, what the hell? From the far distance of New York, I had cried for dialogue. Well, here it was offered, in the very heartland of racism. He'd said that native Blacks would very likely treat an overture to friendliness with suspicion and distrust. He didn't say how they would treat a dare, a challenge. I'd come this far to see and hear for myself, from anyone who would show me and tell me. Would I reject such an invitation if it came from a liberal or a Black?

"Okay," I said to him.

"Then you'll come?"

"Yes. I'll come."

Soon after we sat down to dine. The banker excused himself and left. Now the conversation shifted to other things, gas shortage, the state of the economy, the imminent elections, etc. Like any other dinner party anywhere. Relaxed with them, I enjoyed the food, the company, the talk, but from time to time would pull myself up wondering if it was all a special exercise in good manners for my benefit. Impossible. They were talking among themselves in a familiar, ordinary way. My being there imposed no strain upon them. I'd have to watch myself and not let my blackness become my own handicap.

3

About nine o'clock there was a call for me from a friend of a friend in England. I'd spoken to him earlier and mentioned that I would be dining at Helen's. Now he phoned to let me know that he'd arranged for me to meet a group of people and, if I wished, he'd come to the Suzman home to fetch me. I agreed.

In London and New York, friends had said, "While you're in South Africa, you must meet so-and-so, a really fine person who could be very helpful to you over there. I'll give you his (her) phone number and drop him (her) a line to say you'll be in touch." I've never been very enthusiastic about that sort of introduction, and was even less so in the case of South Africa. My friends in New York and London were white and the introductions were to white South Africans. Were they really liberal or would they put on an act of liberalism for the sake of their distant friends? So far, Helen was everything that had been claimed for her. I'd soon find out about John.

He arrived about an hour later and I left with him. On the way to his home, he told me that the people he'd invited to meet me were all involved in the arts—in an amateur way, because there was little opportunity for them professionally. The arts were still struggling in South Africa, and though there were rich veins of talent running throughout the society, too little attempt was made to tap and promote them. As we drove, he pointed out places of local interest, mostly new multistoried buildings, and commented on the elaborate highway system under development.

At his home, I met his wife, two teenaged sons, and his other guests, all men, four black and one white. I was quite surprised, perhaps foolishly so, because he'd given no hint of their color, but spoke merely of artists. At Helen's, the only other Blacks in sight were servants. Judging by the large living room, the house was commodious, but the shabbily comfortable furniture suggested a modest budget. I wondered what John did for a living; his strong handclasp in greeting had been made with a calloused hand, hinting at outdoor work. What was his relationship to these Blacks and how was he able to bring them together at such short notice?

The family and guests welcomed me. I wondered how I should approach the black men, my memory of my encounter in the park bidding caution, so I expressed my pleasure at being in their country and hoped they would take it from there.

"My name's Obie and this is James and Kebo and Molefe. We've all read at least one of your books, *To Sir, with Love*. When we heard from John here that you were here, we agreed to take a chance and stay in town a little later to meet you."

"Take a chance?" I asked. "What do you mean?"

"Didn't you know? Blacks are not allowed in the city at night," he replied, his easy smile sugarcoating the words.

"So where do you live?"

"We all live outside the city in a place they created for

us called Soweto. But tell us, what are you doing in this place? John wouldn't give us any details."

"I'm just visiting," I replied.

"Did you know that your books were banned here?" the one named Molefe asked. He was short, stocky, with a shiny, hairless head and tiny curls on his upper lip and chin. The total effect was a little startling, as if he would be more at home on a pirate ship with a cutlass held between his large, white teeth.

"Yes. I knew."

"What we've been wondering," Molefe continued, "is why they issued you a visa after banning your books."

"The ban was lifted," I replied. "There was an announcement in the *Official Gazette.*" They were making me feel uncomfortable; the warmth of their greeting had quickly evaporated. I looked at John, wondering whether he had deliberately set this up. Hell, I'd never met him before tonight and he had knowingly brought me into this. Since entering his house, he'd retreated into the background, saying nothing, leaving it to the others to grill me. His wife sat on a divan with her sons, silent, observing.

"Makes no difference, man," Obie interposed. "The things you say in your books remain. I read *Reluctant Neighbors.* No white man is going to love you for that one and no South African White would forgive you for even thinking such things. So we want to know if the ban was lifted after you applied for a visa."

"No. I saw the notice of the lifting of the ban and then inquired about the visa."

"Did you have any trouble getting it?"

"I wouldn't call it trouble. When I learned that the ban was lifted I spoke with the South African Consul General in New York. He suggested that I formally apply for a visa to test the lifting of the ban on my books. I waited about five months after applying, then I learned that the visa was granted."

"As easy as that? No restrictions, no limitations?" Obie was slim, in a neat dark suit, and soft spoken with an easy, intellectual air. He chose his words carefully, as if weighing each one to insure its fullest impact. His heavy-lidded eyes always seemed half closed.

"When the visa came through, I arranged to see the Consul General and asked whether, if I visited his country, I would be allowed to move about freely and talk with persons black and white. He assured me that I'd have no difficulty in either respect. After giving the matter considerable thought, I decided to make the visit and here I was."

"As easy as that?" from Obie again.

"As easy as that," I answered.

"Doesn't it tell you anything, man?" Molefe asked. "Your books were banned. The film of the first one was first banned, then released but restricted to White-only bijous*.. They ban the works of people they consider dangerous, or they consider the works dangerous, whatever way you look at it. They go to all that trouble against you and then hand you a visa. Doesn't it tell you anything?"

"They're using you, man," the deep, resonant voice of Kebo intervened. He was big, his bulk further emphasized by the bulge of his belly under the loose-fitting, short-sleeved caftan. A tiny golden earring fitted snugly into the lobe of his left ear. A large, handsome man, I could imagine him a fierce Othello.

"I don't agree." They were getting to me, stirring up resentments I didn't imagine I'd feel against fellow Blacks. Did they think I was some kind of cretin? In New York, I'd

*Cinemas.

asked myself all these questions and more. Not only about the banned books, but about my United Nations speeches and statements as well. These men were suggesting that the lifting of the ban on my books was a deliberate ploy to entice me into visiting South Africa! By implication they were crediting the South African Government not only with the highest intelligence, but with prescience as well. I didn't buy that.

"Think about it," he went on. "They ban your books and your film. Okay. Now they lift the ban and give you a visa. No restrictions. Ergo, South Africa is pursuing more liberal policies, see? They let you in, a black man with an international reputation as a critic of racist and discriminatory policies. That means something, man. It's like Arthur Ashe playing in their tennis tournament and Bob Foster fighting their lily-white champion. Liberal South Africa." He made a brushing gesture with his large hand as if to erase an unwelcome vision.

"I'm here because I wanted to come here," I said. "If your Government so cleverly anticipated my moves, so what? I'm still in charge of my own eyes and ears. I'm still in control of my own mind."

"Happy to hear it," said Obie.

"Famous last words," from Molefe, a sly grin pulling down one side of his mouth. Okay, if these bastards were playing some game, I'd had enough of it. I looked at John, but he refused to meet my eye.

"Where are you living?" James asked. He had been sitting all the while in a large overstuffed chair which seemed to hold his tiny body captive. In the deepest chair, in the darkest corner of the room, he'd become inconspicuous and now I could see little more than the narrow face. However, I was grateful for his intervention.

"I'm staying at the Landdrost."

"That's the new hotel on Plein Street opposite the park," John said.

"Bob Foster stayed there," Molefe said.

"Do you plan to write a book about South Africa, after your visit?" Obie asked, smiling his soft smile.

"It's very possible."

"How do you plan to see the country and the people? Will you just wander around by yourself or will you be shown, officially?"

"Whichever way will help me see what I want to see," I said. "I was told in New York that the Information Office would give me any help I need. I'd be very grateful if any of you can give me any leads." Maybe I was missing something here. Could be that these fellows were trying to be helpful, in their own way. What was it Helen Suzman had said about them not trusting me? Maybe that was it. Perhaps they'd learned to be damned careful, even with other Blacks. Well, they had a perfect right to question my motives, but I wished it could have been done in a more friendly manner.

"The Information Office!" he exclaimed. "So you'll be given the conducted tour and shown only what they want you to see. The white tour. Then you'll go back to where you come from and say South Africa's a lovely place."

"Look, I'm a stranger here. I don't know my way around, so I'll have to depend on someone to tell me things. If you don't trust the official line, why don't you help? Why don't you show me what you think I ought to see?"

"The Landdrost is a far cry from the way Blacks live in this country," Kebo chimed in.

"I have no choice but to stay at the Landdrost."

"Why don't we cut the shit and tell our brother what

it's really like to be black in this place. If he's willing to listen. After all, he's come to see us, so let's tell him what it's like to be treated like shit in the land of his forefathers." Kebo stood up, looking large and threatening as the light caught the shiny smoothness of his massive forearms. "I read your book, my brother. It hurt you when you couldn't get the job you wanted, because of your black skin. You think that's something? Here you won't even be allowed to apply. Here, no Black would dare raise his ambitions that high. Any job higher than shit carrier is reserved for the white man. By law."

Reaching under his caftan into a pocket of his trousers he produced a flat, worn little book and flicked it open before my face.

"This is what every black man and woman is reduced to in this place. This thing. It governs our lives. Because of it, you're nothing. Without it, you're less than nothing. Man, you could leave your country thousands of miles away and come here, just because you wanted to see how we live! All you needed was a visa. We can't move a single step without this thing, day or night."

I wanted to take a closer look at the thing he held under my nose, but thought it unwise to interrupt him. His anger was all the more powerful because it was so controlled.

"Listen, brother," he said, "John got in touch with us today and told us you were in town. We wanted to meet you, to meet a black brother who can come and go as he pleases, write as he pleases, think as he pleases. But when we meet you, we realize how it is possible to live differently from the way we are. We give you some shit because we are angry at the difference between you and us. Christ, even to meet you we have to creep about in the dark like criminals. We are here in John's house. When it's time to go, do you think we can just walk out the door? No. However late it is, John will have to take us out of the city to Soweto where we live."

"Why?" I asked, directing the question to John, wanting to hear from him about it. Before he could reply, Molefe said, "Any Black found in the city after eleven o'clock at night is in trouble. The police cruise around in vans looking for Blacks. Only a few house servants or restaurant employees or watchmen are allowed here at night; they have special permission obtained by their employers. For any other, it's into the van and off to the police station."

"Even if you have one of those books?" I pointed to the one which Kebo still held in his hand.

"Yes. Even if you have the Book. That only permits you to be in the city by daylight. Not at night. It's called the Book of Life. Here, take a look at mine."

He handed it to me. It was a thin group of printed forms stapled together inside a black leatherette cover and arranged alphabetically as follows:

Page A.   Residential address:
Permit to be employed in Johannesburg daily from 8 A.M. to 11 P.M.

Page B.   Reserved for monthly signature of employer.

Page C.   Poll tax stamps.
        (*Poll tax must be paid by June of each year.*)

Page D.   Homeland tax stamps.
        (*Rated according to individual's earnings.*)

Page E.   Bantu Labour Health Regulations.

Page F.   Driver's license.

Page G.   Reserved for Arms License.
(*This is a mockery as no arms licenses are issued to Blacks. Any Black found in possession of even a penknife is liable to arrest and prosecution.*)

Page H. Personal particulars, including those of wife and children, if any.

Page I. Reserved for photograph of individual.

"Think of it, my friend," Molefe continued. "You walk free. Every one of us Blacks, from the age of sixteen, must carry one of these at all times. Without it you have no identity, no life, so you spend your life safeguarding it."

"Do you know what's one of the most humiliating acts of my life?" Obie said. "Getting my Book signed each month. It says that it should be signed by the employer, but that really means that any white man can sign it, and the signing is usually assigned to the most junior white in the job. Boy, and do they shit on you! They're so happy to have someone below them, they make you crawl for that signature. And I crawl, my brother. Me, who would love to take them by the throat, I crawl for that signature. In your book, *Reluctant Neighbors*, you talk of pride as if it is every man's birthright. Here the black man has no birthright, not even the pride in being a man."

"You asked me earlier how I planned to move around and learn about conditions. I'll see what the officials want to show me, but I'd like to hear from you and other Blacks, too, about conditions as you see them, if you'd be willing to talk to me and show me."

"Only if you're prepared to come and see us where we live," Molefe replied. "We can't come often to John's house. Too risky for him and his family. Before you know it the Security Police will be on to him for consorting with Blacks. They'll think we're plotting something. In any case, it would be better to show you how we live than merely tell you about it. Think your stomach can stand it?"

"Certainly. If yours can."

John's wife and children served some cool drinks and the discussion switched to other things. Mainly writing. Poetry. Now I discovered that the white guest, Brian, was involved in publishing and promoting the works of black authors and poets in South Africa. Without a white person to help, Blacks had no access to the publishing houses. Obie, whose recently published book of poems had been very well received, was particularly bitter about this.

"In every way, at every turn, we're made and kept dependent on the white man. Brian here's okay, but why should we have to need even him? Whites come along and claim to be interested in our poetry, novels and plays and promise to act on our behalf. Then they promote our work for their own benefit, they complete the negotiation without a word to us, they give us what they choose. They know we can't fight them in the courts. God, let our day come!"

The Whites seemed quite unmoved by these outbursts as if they'd either heard them all before or were confident that they occupied a separate and different place in the Blacks' regard. Perhaps people like John, his family, and Brian represented a bridgehead of interracial trust and understanding. Maybe there were others like him. John's surname suggested that he was of Boer stock. His hands were rough and calloused by hard work. How did he manage to win the trust of Blacks like these bright, intelligent men? How deep and real was his liberal stance? His children seemed comfortable in the company of Blacks, and children of that age are usually an excellent barometer of a family's racial attitudes. Christ, there was so much to be learned and so little time. I'd planned to stay six weeks and already that seemed too short.

On my way to the hotel that night, driven by John's wife, I saw two of the police vans making their rounds;

mobile gray boxes already heavy with the nightly haul. There, I thought, but for the grace of God . . .

Next morning, I was up early—the noise of traffic from the street below nudged me awake. I showered, breakfasted, and I decided to take a stroll, perhaps to window-shop for some small memento of my visit to this city. At a street intersection near the hotel, a police minicar stood by the curb. I crossed the road, giving no more than a fleeting glance to the burly, red-faced officer at the wheel, and made my way slowly down the block, pausing outside a fruitstand to admire the racked display boxes laden with luscious fruit. Yellow mangoes, dark purple plums, large tight bunches of black grapes, red flecked yellow peaches nestling in pockets of soft paper, pears, grapefruit, bananas, nectarines, all looking so fresh and delectable. Two dark-skinned men, Indians, waited courteously on the customers. I wondered if the Indians owned the shop or merely worked there, and promised myself to buy some of the fruit on my way back.

A little farther along, I stopped to watch a construction site across the street. Blacks and Whites pulling and carrying, hammering and drilling amid the noise and bustle, the towering naked girders and the swinging crane cables. From where I stood, there seemed to be harmony on that job, the natural, active interdependence I'd observed on building sites in New York, London, or Paris. I'd inquire about it. I noticed that the policeman was approaching on foot from the right, jackbooted and helmeted, the leather thongs from a thick club dangling beside his right leg, his face anonymous behind large dark goggles.

Huge, powerful, and casual, he seemed to be walking directly toward where I stood. I wondered if I should move out of his way, but quickly rejected the idea. Hell, the sidewalk was wide enough for both of us and more. In New York, black petitioners had told of brutal treatment at the hands of the South African police. One had said to me, "The police come along and toss you into their car and take you to the police station. They ask you questions and you must remember to say '*Baas*,' each time you answer. If you don't, they beat you across the mouth with their short clubs to teach you how to speak to a white man." Blacks aren't allowed to say Yes and No. They must always show proper humility to the white *Baas*. Fascinated, I watched him approach. As he came nearer and nearer, I felt nervous, fearful flutterings in my gut and sudden perspiration ran coldly down my armpits. Good sense told me to move, step back or forward, but stubbornness made me stay where I was.

I felt afraid, awed by the towering faceless size of him, until it was too late to move; I braced myself for the inevitable crunching contact—but suddenly, nimbly, he sidestepped away from me and continued his slow, deliberate way until he was out of sight.

Later, I mentioned the near-incident in a telephone conversation with a friend who advised me to do the safe thing in the future and give way, unless I wanted a brutal beating with no redress. He reminded me that the policeman would have no way of knowing that I was an overseas visitor and would merely consider my behavior another instance of "kaffir cheek" which deserved whatever it got, and no one, Black or White, would intervene on my behalf. I could easily be hauled off to the nearest police station and humiliated before any attempt was made to identify me, my unfamiliar accent notwithstanding.

I paid a courtesy call at the Office of Information to let the officials know I had arrived in Johannesburg and to find out what formalities I would have to go through to achieve my purpose, learning about the lives of Blacks. I was courteously received and told that the information offices in every city would be happy to facilitate my inquiries in every way. No formalities were necessary except when I wished to visit the black enclaves in or near the major cities. For entry into these a special police pass was required. This pass, I was told, was intended for my own protection; the crime rate in those enclaves was very high, and the authorities were concerned for my safety. I thanked the Information Officer and expressed the wish then and there to visit Soweto, the largest black township within the immediate environs of Johannesburg. I was promptly given permission, together with a guide, an employee of the Information Office, and promised a comprehensive look at every facet of life in the black community. I was told that my guide, a blonde young woman, was very knowledgeable about Soweto and would be able to answer any question put to her about the township and its inhabitants. A white guide to inform me about the living conditions of blacks in a Black enclave in which not even a single White lived or was allowed to live? What would she really know? I'd wait and see.

Soweto is the largest of several black townships within the jurisdiction of Johannesburg, about fifteen miles outside the city and far enough away for the Whites not to be offended by its ugliness or threatened by the violence which frequently erupts there. It is situated in a natural hollow, the inhabitants restricted to an area of approximately thirty-four square miles. There is only one road in or out, wide and hard-surfaced to the edge of the township, and readily blocked off and controlled if necessary.

"What's the population of Soweto?" I asked my guide as we stopped briefly on a rise overlooking the township, the low, tightly packed, box-like white houses glimmering

in the sunny heat, and reminiscent of the packed grave-
yards between Manhattan and La Guardia Airport.

"About six hundred thousand."

She had the figure pat and ready for me. Hadn't I
heard somewhere that Blacks in South Africa did not vote
and no official census was taken of them? As if it had served
its intended purpose, the hard-surfaced road ended abruptly at the entrance to Soweto, opposite the huge General
Hospital. From there on into the township, the road was
pitted and worn, with deep ruts holding water from some
recent rain. Now we came upon row upon row of prefabri-
cated four-roomed concrete houses, built closely together
and separated from each other by a narrow grassy alleyway
into which grew a few trees or shaggy shrubs. Some of
these houses were roofed in concrete while others had
corrugated galvanized metal roofs which caught and reflected the sunlight. Each house was fitted with four small
windows and a door. I guessed that there was a window for
each room, but those gleaming roofs worried me.

"What's it like inside?" I asked my guide. "In this heat
it must be really awful."

"Not really," she replied. "They're designed to stay
cool in summer and warm in winter."

"How?"

"Something to do with the way they're built," she
replied lamely.

"Have you ever been in one?"

"No, but I've talked with some builders on the
project."

We stopped the car so that I could take a closer look at
one of the houses. I saw no sign of electric cables or the
familiar exhaust outlet which indicated internal sewerage.

"What about electric lighting?" I asked her.

"Most of the houses are fitted with electricity," she

replied. "Some of these older ones are without, but the plan is to extend it to all of them. The houses in this section are among the first built in Soweto. You can tell that because many of them have the old concrete roofs. The locals call them sleeping elephants. The newer ones are a real improvement. They have electricity and running water. The older ones have outdoor water taps."

Ten or fifteen years earlier, she went on, Soweto was a terrible slum and the Government, in its concern for the welfare of the inhabitants, had embarked on a comprehensive rehousing scheme. From time to time, the scheme was revised and improvements included. But inevitably housing needs outstripped the pace of construction. As new houses were built, the slums were bulldozed out of existence and their occupants relocated. The houses could be bought or rented. When they were bought, the purchase related only to the building, not to the land. In Soweto and similar black townships, the house may be bought but the land on which it stands can only be leased. The length of such a lease is usually less but never more than thirty-five years, and this period may be extended or not, at the discretion of the authorities. If an extension of his lease is denied, the black lessee has no hope of appeal. My guide supplied these interesting pieces of information matter-of-factly. There was nothing bitter or vengeful about her statements or observation; she was merely providing information on a state of affairs which exists, and she was in no way personally involved.

Tenants, she informed me, fared no better. A house is rented to an individual who occupies it with his family, usually a wife and three or four small children. That is the "official" family. Because there are not enough houses to accommodate in comfort even sixty percent of those needing shelter, subletting is encouraged and practiced. The tenant benefits little from this, however, for subtenants must pay their rent, not to him, the "official" tenant, but to the landlord, the city of Johannesburg, through its local agent. It can be assumed that there is hardly a house in Soweto without its quota of subtenants, so considerable revenues must accrue to the city over and above the basic rents anticipated for the scheme.

I asked her if she could arrange for me to look inside one of the houses, but she merely smiled at that. Actually, I could not see her approaching any of those black residents. Many of the women interrupted their chores long enough to stare at us, my blonde guide and me. I wondered what they thought of us.

As the tour progressed, there was no escaping the drab sameness of the houses, the garbage-littered streets, or the few shoddy shops. Groups of youths sat outside the shops or wandered about aimlessly. My guide explained that the schools were still out for the long Christmas vacation. She pointed out what she called some of the special advantages of Soweto. Picnic grounds, a pleasantly green though unkempt oasis; a large football stadium where all the main outdoor social and athletic events, such as boxing matches, were held; a nursery school for children of working mothers; the empty Soweto High School. We pulled into the high school yard and I peeped into a classroom through a broken window. Row upon row of dusty wooden desks, the walls unrelieved by even a map. Gloomy.

Our tour continued along roads now generally tar-surfaced and comfortably passable and we stopped at the only vocational school in Soweto. About two hundred youths annually, as many as the school can now accommodate, are selected out of more than a thousand who have passed a qualifying examination, and are taught the rudiments of electrical wiring, plumbing, bricklaying and masonry, and carpentry.

The school's principal was an Englishman long resident in South Africa, and, like most school principals, complained of the acute shortage of basic equipment, materials, and textbooks, in spite of which the youths were making extraordinary progress. I saw some of the models made by the students and some of their drawings, and they compared very favorably with work I'd seen by design students in well-equipped classrooms in London and New York. One student's work was so outstanding that a visiting Swiss diplomat had given him a very expensive watch in encouragement.

The Principal said that, given the opportunity and further training, the black students could excel in the building and other industries which are clamoring for skilled labor. Unfortunately, they are victimized by South Africa's "job reservation" laws, by which all skilled and some semiskilled jobs are reserved to Whites. A bricklayer, plasterer, or electrician must be white. The young black students, ambitious and enthusiastic while training, face a very frustrating future. They are likely to be employed as low-paid helpers to Whites less skilled than themselves and might even do the work without receiving the pay.

The Principal told me that present building needs have forced some builders to let Blacks do skilled work, even at the risk of prosecution. Reflecting a booming economy, contractors are enjoying their busiest times and there is an acute shortage of skilled white labor. There are many Blacks on their payrolls fully capable of skilled work without supervision. To meet their pressing deadlines, the contractors put the Blacks on skilled jobs and keep legal representation readily available to deal with such prosecution and fines as are incurred. Legal fees and fines are prorated into each building estimate. The Principal hoped that, eventually, the job reservation laws would crumble under pressure from public need for housing and the industry's need to expand.

We now drove through the so-called elite section of the town. Most of the homes here were attractive bungalows surrounded by neatly trimmed lawns, with flowering shrubs and fruit trees. These were the homes of Soweto's tiny "black bourgeois" community, the local doctor, dentist, grocer, gas-station operator, etc., all of whom had struggled and saved to rise above the depressing sameness. Each of them had begun by buying the government-built four-room square structure and added rooms to it as they could. They had had to install at their own expense running water, plumbing facilities, electricity, and whatever other household devices they could afford. All this on a flimsy lease which could be rescinded at the Government's whim.

Ironically, my guide spoke of the bungalows and their owners proudly, as if those people had been specially "allowed" to achieve that much, her voice crisp and objective as if she were speaking of cold, inanimate things, not insecure human beings who were forced to live in fear that one fine day the dreams they'd earned would be snatched away from them. I thought of myself, my own pride in ownership of a home thousands of miles away, my security in the knowledge that I had the right to defend it against all comers, supported by the full weight of the law.

My guide now promised a big surprise and we drove to the Bantu Council Building. It was much more than a surprise, the sight of that modern red-brick building, graceful in its simple lines against a dramatic background of neatly trimmed lawns and darkening sky. A macadam driveway circled in front of the building before coming to rest at the base of a wide wooden stairway which led upward to carved wooden doors. A uniformed doorman led us inside and then hurried away to find the Secretary of the Council. My guide proudly showed me the large Council Chamber, paneled in wood and thickly carpeted, and the smaller offices of the President and Secretary of the Council.

We found the Secretary in his office in conversation with someone, so we waited for him in the Council Chamber. My guide told me that members of the Council are mainly drawn from the small business community of Soweto. The Council is supposed to oversee Soweto's health and educational and social welfare, and make recommendations to the white Johannesburg Council which has the final decision as to which, if any of them, are expedited.

When the Council Secretary finally joined us, he proceeded to give me a very careful review of the Council and its work. He seemed primarily concerned with impressing my guide whom he knew to be a Government official. Smiling broadly, he invited me to ask him questions.

"How much freedom can your Council exercise in the management of Soweto's affairs?" I asked.

"Well," glancing nervously at my guide, "we have a pretty free hand. We're on the spot, we know what the township needs, and our recommendations are generally honored." Nodding his head affirmatively all the while.

"Does the Council collect the rents on the houses?"

"Yes."

"Would you tell me about subletting and how it works here?"

"Well, I couldn't go into that. That's the Council's business. I can't discuss that."

"I understand you maintain supervision of the schools."

"Yes."

"I've just been looking at your high school. From the outside—"

"The schools are still out for the Christmas holidays," he interrupted.

"I know. But could you—"

"The Chairman of the Schools Committee would be the best person to talk to you about the schools." Again he interrupted me, anticipating my question, meanwhile looking at my guide as if to assure her that he would say or do nothing contrary to official policy.

Unexpectedly we were joined by a little man, hardly over five feet tall, shiningly bald, and spry. On being introduced to me, he seemed surprised.

"I thought you were a plainclothes policeman," he said. "I was planning to ask you to help me get a new pass." Grinning meanwhile.

"At your age, why would you need a pass?" I asked him.

"Every black man needs a pass," he replied, the smile vanishing. "I am a member of this Council. I live and work here in Soweto. Been here nearly all my life. I'm seventy and still I need a pass." His watery eyes staring balefully at my guide, he continued, "Blacks are not human, so they need passes to move among the humans. What about you?"

"I'm a visitor from overseas. This is my first visit to your country and this lady is guiding me around Soweto."

"Before people try to guide others, they should try guiding themselves," he replied, looking at me. "How can you guide when you don't know Soweto yourself? Blacks live in Soweto. Only Blacks. They're forced to live in Soweto. They know what is Soweto. The white man comes here and says to us, Come. Go. Fetch. Carry. Live. Die. Show your permit. Show your pass. That's all the white man knows about Soweto. Busloads of white tourists drive through the township with somebody in the bus showing them how the Bantu live. Somebody white, from the Information Office. They say, 'Look at the Bantu, how happy they are in Soweto. Look at them smile. Look at the happy children playing football. Look at the happy old men drinking Bantu beer.' Guides!"

He made the last word sound like an insult, speaking his mind, careless of any effect it might have on the now pale white woman. The Council Secretary nervously wet his lips from time to time as if preparing to intervene, but the old one seemed beyond caring, beyond fear. Perhaps, I thought, he has finally come to terms with himself, his life and his dignity, and has decided to make his stand.

"You want to see Soweto, come to us," he told me. "Come as a brother."

I apologized for the impromptu visit, saying that my stay in Johannesburg was short and I'd taken advantage of the opportunity provided me to see his township. But he would not be pacified.

"If you want to know about us, make time. Don't tell me you have too little time. You're one of us, black like us. You do not need any White to tell you about us or show you how we live. We'll make time to see you, talk with you. Let us know when you can come, but come. We need to meet our brothers from far away. You've come this far, don't tell me you have no time."

I felt humbled and promised that I'd make the time to be with them. Somehow. He was good for me. I felt elated, and at the same time, reminded of my priorities.

That was the end of my guided tour. On the way back to Johannesburg, my guide and I talked, but desultorily. She seemed to have lost much of her enthusiasm. At my hotel, there were telephone calls for me from a local newspaper, the *Johannesburg Times*, seeking an interview, and from a black poet I'd met. I returned the *Times* call and agreed to be interviewed, then called the poet and, in passing, mentioned that I'd just made a guided tour of Soweto. He laughed at the idea of the white guide and suggested that it was a deliberate ploy on the part of the Office of Information to keep me away from the inhabitants of Soweto. He himself offered to take me there or anywhere else so that I could really meet the people. I told him that I'd been warned not to go into a township without a permit, but he brushed that aside, asking who the hell would know the difference. I'd be a black man in a black township. "They say we all look alike, don't they?" he laughed. I agreed to take the risk and go with him.

4

On the appointed day, we met in front of the hotel and drove to Alexandra, six miles outside of the city in the opposite direction from Soweto. We drove through lovely suburbs of wide, clean streets and charming villas surrounded by neat lawns and carefully nurtured hedges and the ubiquitous blue-tinted swimming pool. All along the route were the separate bus stops for Blacks and Whites.

My first impression of Alexandra was of a garbage dump. Everywhere the garbage was piled as if the inhabitants had long given up the struggle to remove it and just let it accumulate. Where Soweto had roads and drearily similar box-like houses, Alexandra had a jumble of narrow, garbage-clogged foot paths worn out of the naked earth by decades of footsteps, intersecting with shallow gullies which wound their way erratically here and there until they were lost in sudden overgrowths of weeds. What had once long ago been neat houses had deteriorated into dilapidated wrecks patched with tin, cardboard, or even strips of plastic, their squalor emphasized by the uglier little tin outhouses scattered around them. In the middle of all this, two buildings rose ten or twelve stories into the air, straight sided, red-bricked, and looking clinically functional, as if contemptuous of the squalor though firmly anchored in it.

These were the hostels, one for men and one for women, built to house cheap black labor necessary for the numerous manpower-hungry industrial projects which are mushrooming around Johannesburg. They were designed to accommodate the largest number of workers in the least possible space, and are a honeycomb of tiny, cell-like rooms. Cold running water and toilets are provided at one central location in each building.

Most of the black workers in Johannesburg and its environs are young men born in ghettos like Soweto and Alexandra; others are migrant workers from the Bantustans of the Transvaal, Transkei, Zululand, and other outlying territories, or immigrants from Rhodesia, Botswana, Lesotho, Swaziland, and even Mozambique. These migrant and immigrant workers are not permitted to travel with their wives, and see them for only a short time each year, at Christmas, when they are given leave to return home.

"Well, what do you think of all this?" my companion asked.

"It stinks," I replied, meaning the garbage.

"What about those?" pointing to the hostels.

"At least they're an improvement on the tin shacks around them."

"You think so? Talk to some of the fellows who live in them. Best that can be said of them, they have electricity and running water. They'd never house white men in places like that."

"Could I take a look?"

"Doubt it. They don't encourage outsiders. We could peep in if you like. Many of the ground floor rooms have broken windows and nobody seems to be in any hurry to repair them."

I declined, not wanting to intrude on the hostel residents, but my friend led the way through the weeds and stunted trees to the base of one of the hostels.

"This is the women's unit," he said. "All these lower rooms are empty. Peeping Toms and things like that, you know. And besides, most of the women stay in the hostel only for a short while then try to find jobs as domestics with the chance of living in their employers' houses."

I looked through one of the broken windows. The narrow room contained a small iron cot with a thin, plastic-covered mattress. A rickety wooden table completed the furniture.

"The men's hostel is always filled to capacity, with a waiting list of others wanting to get in," he said.

"Where do they live while they're waiting?"

"You really want to see?"

He led me back toward the shacks and we had to pick our way over piles of garbage and around a partly enclosed but uncovered hole which evidently served as the communal lavatory. There was a water spigot a few yards away. We entered one of the ramshackle houses and he knocked on an inner door, then pushed it open to let us into a pitiful room about eight foot square. Although we had come in from bright sunlight the room was in near total darkness; the only window was tightly sealed with burlap. A young man crouched by a single lighted candle, eating something with his fingers from a metal pot. My companion made the introduction, but, in the circumstances, no attempt was made to shake hands. I could not see the young man's face clearly in the prevailing gloom and I knew he could not see mine. He sat on the edge of a cot, one of three which ringed the room. He told us that six of them, five other men and himself, lived there, sleeping two to a cot. I tried to imagine what it was like.

The young man finished his meal, wiped his fingers with a piece of paper and stood up. I saw that he was neatly dressed in short, sharply creased slacks and shiny shoes. He said he was employed as a clerk with a local engineering firm, having graduated from the Orlando High School in Soweto. He suggested that we leave as he had arranged to meet some of his friends nearby. As we were leaving, I noticed that another of the cots was occupied, someone making the most of having the entire cot to himself. No electricity, no running water, no sewage facilities, no privacy, no sunlight, no air.

"Christ!" the word slipped out.

"Getting to you, eh?" my friend said. "I sometimes read about how you black Americans riot because of your living conditions. We'd trade with you any day, and think ourselves lucky. How long do you think you'd remain human in a room like that? You can hardly close your eyes before there's someone wanting to stick it up your ass. Hell, no women available, so what can you expect. The women who live here stay indoors at night. Rape around here is less a crime than a daily hazard."

"Don't these fellows ever take any action?"

"Action? What action? In this country you work or you starve. If you have a job you hang onto it because you know that there are several others just waiting for you to slip. Action? You mean like striking? Shit, they'd throw you in jail so fast! Don't forget you're talking about Blacks."

God, no wonder the white guide had kept far away from this place! These black men and women act- ually had to pay to stay in stinkholes like this. Somebody was making a fortune out of all this misery and it wasn't the

Blacks. They could not own property, thus could not be landlords. So it had to be either the Government, through its Bantu Councils, or private industry, growing fat on Government contracts.

"We welcome evolution but we are opposed to revolution." The banker had repeatedly chanted the Government's slogan. So had the MP, Englebrecht. Didn't they realize that it was in places like this that revolutions were born and bred? Maybe they'd never seen sights like these, even though they festered right under their very eyes. In other places, others had been similarly blind and uncaring until someone had rubbed their insensitive noses in the shit.

My friend led me on through the darkening township. I felt that he was slyly pleased at the way I had been affected by the hostel visit, and how carefully I was stepping around the mounds of garbage in our path. People sat on the stoops of the shacks chatting with each other, seeming unmindful of the ugly chaos around them.

"How would you like to spend a week or two here?" He was smiling. Laughing at me.

"Not for anything," I answered. I wanted to get away from there, away from the stench, the dilapidation, the all-pervading air of decay. It was getting me down. I couldn't understand how he could be so at ease, so comfortable. Then I remembered this was what he wrote about in his poems.

"A bit different from your guided tour of Soweto, isn't it?" he grinned. "The Information Office never brings tourists down here. No smooth roads for the cars, no fancy playgrounds for happy, smiling black children. No Government show pieces. All we have is what you see. Decay and death, and we're forced to live in it. Nowhere to move to, and even if we found somewhere better, how the hell would we get permission to move? You saw what the inside of that hostel unit looked like? Some rooms in these other places are worse. Much worse. And people live here and rear their children. Right here in these miserable holes. Christ Almighty, it's inhuman!"

"I agree," I told him.

"You agree!" He suddenly turned on me, the thin face tight with anger, a trickle of spittle escaping his mouth. "You agree! That's mighty big of you, my friend. But in a few minutes you'll walk away from it, back to your fancy hotel. I suppose you'll take a nice hot bath and wash away every memory of this stinking slum. You agree! That's nice. That's very nice. We agree too, but we still have to live in this shit. And pay for the privilege. Do you realize that? We pay rent to live in these stinking, rotten holes. Come with me, man. There's something else you should see!"

With that he started off down a narrow alleyway between some shacks, not even waiting or looking back to see if I was following him. I hurried after, not daring to risk losing him. He led me beyond the shacks, across an open piece of uneven ground where some kind of dwelling had been bulldozed away, and on to another group of run-down houses, rotting and ready to cave in on themselves. Outside one of these, a very old woman sat in the middle of some cardboard cartons and paper bags filled to bursting with rags. Here my friend stopped and pointed a thin arm.

"Look at her, my friend. She's too old to clean the white man's house or mind his children, so she's discarded, useless as the stinking stuff around her. She can't pay the miserable rent for that shack, so they've thrown her out of it. Look there."

He pointed to the heavy padlock on the rickety door. Unimpressed, uncaring, the aged one sat, staring at nothing in particular, her eyes red and rheumy, her lined face set in final resignation, showing neither pain nor anxiety nor interest in whatever the next unhappy step might be.

"What will happen to her?" I asked.

"If she's lucky she'll die soon," he replied, bitterly. "Maybe someone will take her in for the night. There are lots like her, the white man's garbage. I can show you some more, if you like."

"No, thank you." I was becoming thoroughly irritated with his sneering and his jibes. I'd not created these ugly situations. He'd invited me to come and see, and now he was treating me as if all this was my responsibility.

"Why don't you take her in?" I asked him, striking back.

"Me? Take her where? All I have right now is bed space, and I was damned lucky to find that."

"So we'll both walk away from her, won't we?"

"Yes, my friend, we'll both walk away. But I won't walk far. I can't walk far. I'll always be near enough to see it and hear it and smell it. Every minute of the day it is with me. So I write about it. Me and others like me. We write about the things that hurt us and degrade us, but unlike you, we have no outlets for the things we write. Shit, man, even there we need the white man, and how he exploits our need! But, let's get the hell out of here, if you've had enough." Again he was smiling.

"I've had enough." In silence we returned to Johannesburg.

The next afternoon I went to Dorkay House, a center for the arts in downtown Johannesburg, where I had been invited to hear some black musicians give a private performance for a visiting white American impresario. I was there early and wearily walked up six flights of stairs to a narrow room, with a raised platform at one end, in front of which were rows of metal chairs. The small audience, most of whom were already seated when I arrived, was mostly African with a sprinkling of Whites and Indians who all seemed to know one another. Before the performance began they called to each other in familiar terms, the way artists do everywhere asking about mutual friends, their whereabouts, and whether or not they were working.

The first group to perform, the Batsumi or Hunters, consisted of a flautist, a saxophonist, a pianist, a guitarist, a vocalist who doubled on a huge bongo drum, and two drummers, one who sat enthroned among a glittering assortment of drums and another who beat dexterously on twin, supported kettle drums with padded drumsticks. Two of this group, the kettle drummer and the guitarist, were blind.

From the moment the performance began, it became evident that this was no ordinary group of men. They seemed to enter an immediate dialogue with each other, the pianist provoking the conversational pattern which the others took up, shaped and shaded as their impulses and instruments dictated. With any group, conversational patterns form and re-form. So it was here. They played, or rather they spoke and sang with and through their instruments, many instruments and sounds completely integrated, blending with each other. At times, the flute and saxophone were in private communion, whispering to each other yet providing a variable obbligato to the insistent piano and plaintive guitar. From time to time a musician would break into song, his wordless sounds giving the music an additional, strange dimension.

The flute seemed to be made in two sections, that which contained the mouthpiece being several inches shorter than the shank which held the spaced apertures. Caught in an occasional frenzy of expression, the flautist would pull one part from the other, and, using the palm of one hand as a mute, produce from the truncated instrument extraordinary sounds. At other times, he would blow through the lower part as if it were a trumpet, muttering into it at the same time, this creating a hoarse sound, simultaneously strange and familiar.

From a young woman sitting near me, I learned that they were all from Soweto and were only spare-time musicians; they earned their living as messengers, garage helpers, gardeners, and watchmen. Occasionally they made a recording, but they never received enough from such a venture to make any real difference to their impoverished state.

The second group, the Alan Kinela Quartet, used the same drummers to provide background for a tenor saxophonist and an electric guitarist. Their music was less introspective, more in the familiar, traditional jazz idiom. After a few numbers, this group joined with the first and played *Stumeleng* ("Be Happy"), a lively, exuberant piece from their common tribal heritage.

At the end of the concert, I stayed to meet the musicians. I expressed my delight at the power and joy of their music, all the more impressive in the face of the white South Africans' determined attempts to humiliate and degrade the black man. The vocalist–bongo drummer spoke for the others.

"How is it where you come from?" he asked me. "Where is this place Guyana? In Africa? Where?" His face dripped perspiration which he occasionally scooped away with a forefinger. A handsome young man of medium height, filled with energy which seemed ready to erupt out of him. I told him where Guyana is, pinpointing it on that other continent.

"Tell me about the people," he said. "Are they all

black, like you? Tell me about them." Looking me up and down as if to discover any difference between him and me, them and me.

I told him briefly something of my people. He then asked how long I'd been in Johannesburg, how much I'd seen of the city and the black people and what was my general impression of their condition. Before I could reply, he held up a broad, thick-fingered hand and warned me:

"When you talk about my country, don't pity me. Look at us." Here he moved closer to me as if to emphasize that we were of approximately the same height.

"Talk to us as one of us. I will tell you how I live here and you will tell me about life in your country. I will tell you that I am deeply dissatisfied with the conditions of my life here and perhaps you will tell me that you are dissatisfied with conditions in your own country. We black men have been here for thousands of years. We have learned how to survive the heat and the floods and the drought, the hunger and the times of plenty. Now we must learn to live through slavery, right here in our homeland. We will live through this present experience. Our music is an expression of the spirit, just as survival springs from the spirit, just as hope, love, and strength are things of the spirit. Come, my brothers," he beckoned to the others to come nearer around us. "Come and tell our friend here how we can live in shit and still make music."

His voice had acquired a sharp edge, cutting into me. His round face was grave, the eyes hard, glittering. I guessed his age at twenty-eight or thirty. The voice which had given such poignancy and power to his songs was now low and sonorous, the words tinged with bitterness.

"Tell our friend here that we are of Africa as the dust of the veld and the wind which blows it and as the rivers which are its blood. We are permanently of Africa, as the dust of our fathers is mixed with the dust of the veld. Now we are humiliated here and must bend in the dust. But we will be established again in our rightful place when we learn to pay more attention to things of the spirit. Do you hear me?"

I nodded. I was hearing him.

"I do not speak of your church. I speak of the spirit of man. When we learn, as our fathers did, to pay more attention to things of the spirit, we will know how to work together and suffer together and, once again, be established together in our fatherland."

Abruptly he walked away, the others breaking up to follow him.

Two of his companions, Jim and Joe, remained with me and told me more of their daily lives. They seemed to take it as a matter of course that they would encounter great difficulty in everything.

"Wish we could invite you somewhere for a drink or a cup of coffee," Joe said, "but there is nowhere in this damned city where a black man can buy something even as simple as that. Sorry."

"Don't worry," I told him. "It's enough for me to be able to talk with you. How much do you practice?"

"Oh, we manage about five or six hours a week. We all have jobs here in the city, but we are arrogant enough to believe that we can do better. Much better. Don't you agree?"

"Readily. Listening to you play, now hearing you talk, I've no doubt whatever of your abilities."

"You flatter me, my friend. Say, why don't we get the hell out of this place?" Nodding to Jim and me to follow him out. Downstairs he said, "Wouldn't do much good to talk too much up there. Too many ears listening to everything."

"I'm staying at the Landdrost Hotel not far from here," I told them. "Why don't we go there and have a drink or whatever?"

"That the new big hotel that Bob Foster stayed at?" Jim asked.

"Yes."

"Okay! I'd like to see inside one of those places."

"A hotel is a hotel," I said.

"So speaks the rich American visitor. You're beginning to sound like Bob Foster. You know what that son-of-a-bitch said when he was here? He said that South African Blacks were well off. Said he wouldn't mind buying a house and living here. You know what's funny about that? If he wanted to, he could buy a house here. As an American he would be treated differently. Even if we had the money we are prevented by law from owning land. But they'd let that loud-mouthed bastard buy land if he wanted it. Hell, he's a big-shot boxing champion and he's American."

At the hotel, I noticed their nervousness as they followed me to the desk to collect my key, then up the elevator to my room. We ordered drinks and sat down.

"Christ, just look at me," Joe suddenly exclaimed. "I'm as nervous as a kitten, just coming into this place. A grown man, but the Whites have got me so that I'm scared of my own shadow. Scared to be in their big, shiny hotel even as the guest of a black man like myself. Isn't that too funny, for Christ's sake? What am I? Jesus Christ! What am I?"

"Take it easy, Joe," from Jim.

"Shit with take it easy. He's black like us, so he should understand. Look at me, damn it, look at me and tell me what I am. Our friend here can come into our country, move about as he pleases, live in a hotel like this. In short, he can live as a man. We heard he writes books. He can afford to come all the way here to look at our country and us." Then to me. "Tell me, Mr. Braithwaite, author and VIP, in what way are you different from me?"

"In no way that I can think of," I replied.

"Thank you, my friend, for nothing. Let me tell you a little about me. I have a university degree. From Fort Hare, the black university. That means it is not as good a degree as if I'd had it from a white university. Anyway, that degree suggests that at some time in my life I was ambitious, imaginative, and hopeful. At Fort Hare I used to talk with others like myself, mostly about our hopes and plans for the future. Look at me now. Each day from eight to five, I stack goods in the carrier of a bicycle and deliver them to contemptuous white housewives who never see me, never address me directly. They just point to where they want the stuff put. I've been doing that job for three years and I bet not one of them knows my name."

"Don't think about it," suggested Jim. "We're all in the same boat."

"Think, hell! I don't think about it. To think is to see myself, to recognize the thing I have become in three short years. Sometimes I wish I could kill myself, but what then would become of my wife and two small children? I once read somewhere that prisoners held in solitary confinement spend hours watching ants. I tried that. Do you know what happened? The ant walked away. It had somewhere to go. I have nowhere to go. I no longer think. I am one of the living dead of Soweto."

Listening to him I was hearing myself again. I, too, had thought my situation hopeless.

"What about your music?" I asked, anxious to disperse the painful reflections.

"What about it? Did you enjoy it?"

"Immensely."

"Listen to the man, Joe," Jim said, sarcastically. "He

says he enjoyed our music immensely. What do you think of that? He is able to enjoy, which is a luxury we can't afford. We don't enjoy our music, man. We need it, like an addict needs his *dagga**. It's our survival kit. And there's the other thing. Somebody might like our music well enough to want to do something about it. Cut a record! Arrange a tour! You never know."

Smiling his sad smile as if accustomed to watching his dreams fade and die.

"Shit, man, you never know," said Joe. "Like today. The white men there at Dorkay House. That one in the blue blazer. The bald one. American, I think he is. The other one is local and he told his American friend about us, so he came to listen. Not for nothing. We're tired of performing for them for nothing. He, the American, paid for the session. Anyway, there's always the chance they might like what they hear—"

"Sure, sure," Jim interrupted. "How many times have we gone through that exercise. You know, I've come to the conclusion that I'm mad. Totally mad. Why else would I be sitting here in this fucking hotel where I am not welcome, drinking this man's booze, which is against the law for Blacks, and being what I am not. I could not buy him a stinking cup of coffee, so he brings me here, in this white man's luxury pit, and orders whisky, served to us obsequiously by one like us. It's all madness. I am a human being but I'm restricted to performing menial functions for a miserable pittance. You say, what about my music? I would like to play it and enjoy it, but I play it to relieve myself, not to enjoy. Like the job I do. I don't enjoy it. I just do it and try not to think of it. If I let myself think of it,

*Marijuana.

I'd hate myself and choose to die. I'm dislocated from life. I'm quite mad."

"Don't listen to him," Jim cautioned. "He's as sane as you are, but he gets that way sometimes. A drink or two and he'll snap out of it."

I nodded, but I understood what Joe was saying, because I'd already seen enough to convince me that, forced to live as they were in the ghettos of Soweto and Alexandra, I would surely go mad. Christ, how could anyone feel ambition and hope while restricted to such a stinking environment? Most of the Blacks I'd seen in the city were neatly dressed. How did they manage it? What very special kind of fortitude was required each day and every day in this place to survive an hour, let alone a day? Maybe Joe was right. Maybe madness was the answer.

We spent another hour talking. They were like any black men I'd known in London, New York, Paris, or Jamaica—anywhere. Intelligent, sensitive, and smarting under racial pressure. We had more than enough in common to draw us close together.

I wanted them to be comfortable with me in the only place where we could be together in Johannesburg, but that very comfort was a continuing irritant. They'd come willingly with me, but, once in the room, seemed angry with themselves for being there and angry with me for causing them to be there. They drank, but without conviviality. We'd come up to talk about their music and their lives, but their only comments were on the "white man's luxury" of the hotel and my freedom to enjoy it. I wanted to remind them that I was paying for that suite but decided to keep my mouth shut. Perhaps they were aware of the "Honorary White" thing and were making sly digs at me. What did I have to do to prove that I was with them, sharing their identity? But was I? And what identity? Would I wish to live where they were forced to live, share their lives, suffer the same daily prohibitions and restrictions?

Would I live in Alexandra even for a day? What was my feeling of identity worth if I would not voluntarily share with them? At this level, fine. But what about the levels on which their lives were lived? Could I fetch and carry for the white man and call him *Baas?* The very thought of it sent cold shivers through me. Everything about my life had always pointed in the opposite direction. From childhood.

Into my mind flashed the memory of the Indian cane-cutter named Mungal Sirgh. A white manager on the Berbice sugar estate in Guyana where Mungal Sirgh worked had become impatient with the "lazy coolie bastard" and kicked him. Mungal Sirgh had replied by swinging his machete at the offending leg, slicing through the thick leather and opening the limb neatly from knee to ankle. Taken into custody, his repeated comment was, "He kick me. Kick is for dog. Mungal Sirgh not dog." Christ, why did that come to mind after more than forty years? The "Honorary White" thing was no better than a kick in the ass. The intention was the same. To humiliate the black visitor; to deny him the dignity of his blackness; to remind him that in that society he had no identity except that which they, the Whites, chose to let him have. As a Black I was invisible, not there, not to them. To be seen and heard, I needed an overlay on my invisibility.

If that's how the Whites felt, to hell with them. But what about these men who called me brother? Why was there this gap between us? Perhaps they were saying something to me. Maybe they knew of the Honorary White label and resented it, for my sake. Or maybe they resented me for allowing myself into the situation—a black man labeled white and seeming to enjoy it. I was relieved when they left.

That evening, I asked the hotel doorman to call a taxi to take me to Parktown, a residential suburb of Johannesburg, where I'd accepted an invitation to dine. When the taxi arrived, the doorman opened the door for me and I gave the white driver the address. I could see him eyeing me speculatively in the driving mirror as we got under way. Eventually, he opened up.

"Are you from Botswana?"

"No," I replied.

"Swaziland?"

"No. I'm not African."

"Oh, you're a VIP from overseas." Sounding pleased with himself as if he'd happened on the answer to the sixty-four-thousand-dollar question.

When I paid him, the taxi driver gave me a card with the name and telephone number of his taxi company. At the end of the evening, I telephoned the taxi company and requested a cab to pick me up. I said goodbye to my hosts and waited outside for the cab which soon arrived.

I was about to enter it when the driver called to me.

"Hey you, wait a minute. This is not for you."

"Why not?" I asked.

"This is not for Non-Whites. I'm not allowed to take Non-Whites in this taxi." Meanwhile reaching backward in an attempt to shut the door which I held open.

So, it had happened. After all the fancy official footwork it had happened. Here I was, miles away from the city and without other means of reaching it. I felt suddenly angry at the thought that the taxi would drive away, leaving me there, helpless in an unfamiliar place. On impulse, I climbed in.

"I can't take you," the driver insisted.

"Then we'll damned well both stay here." My anger spilling out. "I telephoned you from this address and you were sent here to collect a passenger and take him to the Landdrost Hotel, weren't you? Well, I'm that passenger and I'll be damned if I'll get out of this taxi." Without another word he turned the vehicle around and headed toward the city.

"If a policeman stops us, I could lose my license," he complained.

"If a policeman stops us, tell him to talk to me!" I responded.

"The bloody dispatcher didn't tell me you were non-white," he went on. "If he'd told me, I'd have known."

"How would he know from the sound of my voice?" I asked.

"Well, non-white VIPs stay at the President or the Landdrost. It's not that I don't want to take Non-Whites in this taxi. It's not me. It's the law. If a policeman stops me with a Non-White in my taxi I could lose my license, and my job. But I suppose it's okay, if you're a VIP."

Just listen to him! This same bastard would have left me stranded back there just because of my black skin.

"Do they ever tell you if a fare is black or white?" I asked.

"Well, no, because we don't normally pick up Non-Whites."

"One of your taxis took me to Parktown from the hotel. In broad daylight, so he knew I was black. He didn't tell me he couldn't carry Blacks. So, if he could carry me there, why all this fuss about taking me back to my hotel? Does the policy of your company change with the drivers or from daylight to night?"

"It's the same policy, but—"

"But you don't want to carry Blacks." I interrupted whatever excuse he was about to give.

"Look, I don't have anything against you—"

"Like hell you don't." In spite of myself the violence was spilling over. "They sent you to pick me up, but one look at this black face and you were ready to fly off and leave me back there in the dark."

"I was only doing my job," I heard him say.

"Hell, no. This is your bloody job. Carrying passengers who call you is your job."

I leaned back, swallowing the rest I wanted to say. What the hell was the use? A bastard like this would do the same thing again five minutes from now. He made some comment, but I didn't hear it. I lost interest in him and anything else he had to say. Just get me to that bloody hotel, I thought. Just get me there.

A few weeks later I learned from the doorman at the Landdrost that some men from the Security Police had been making inquiries about me. They'd questioned the doorman and referred to a comment I'd made to the press about a white taxi driver who'd refused to take me in his cab and had only complied when I'd climbed in over his objections. Apparently they wanted to question the driver and needed some identification from me. They said they would be returning to see me. To hell with them. As far as I was concerned the matter was closed.

The following week, I went to visit a young Indian, living a few blocks from my hotel in a small area temporarily designated "Indian," who recently had been released from the political prison on Robben Island, the same prison in which Chief Nelson Mandela has been held for years. About seven miles offshore from Cape Town, it houses several hundred political dissidents, all black and serving sentences

which range from one to twenty or more years. I was eager
to hear about conditions there at first hand.

The young Indian had been active as a publisher and
distributor of newsletters attacking the Government's racist
policies. He was caught, tried under the Suppression of
Communism Act, and jailed for ten years without right of
appeal. Now, even though he had been released, this young
man was under a restriction order prohibiting him from
having visitors. On entering his house it was agreed that, in
the event of a visit from the police or security agents, I was
to say that I was visiting his brother who lives in the same
house.

He was full-bearded, thin, and hollow-cheeked as if
recently recovered from a long illness, but his handshake
was firm and he greeted me enthusiastically, mainly
because I was from the same country as Dr. Cheddi Jagan
whom he admired tremendously for his resolute position
against the British during Guyana's struggle for independence. He had heard that I was in Johannesburg and
wished to talk with me, to "set me straight," as he put it.
He made reference to the recent visits of Arthur Ashe and
Bob Foster, both of whom, he claimed, played into the
hands of the racist South African Government which
sought to use such visits to divert international pressure
from their policies of segregated sport. He seemed to
believe that any Black from outside who visited South
Africa was, by implication, accepting the prevailing policies as valid. He wanted to know how I had managed to
acquire a visa in the first place and how was it that the
author of a book like *Reluctant Neighbors* could persuade the
South African Government to let him in. He fired off these
and other questions without waiting for answers. He insisted that the Government was deliberately inviting well-
known overseas Blacks, particularly Americans, to South

Africa and showing them certain isolated aspects of the lives of Blacks in the Republic, so as to brainwash them into supporting the Government's racist philosophy. Bob Foster, he said, was a case in point.

"That black American went so far as to state that he liked this country so much he was seriously considering building a house here," he sneered. "The idiot doesn't realize that if he lived here, he, too, would soon be compelled and condemned to live in a black township like Soweto or Alexandra, instead of a fancy suite at the Landdrost Hotel where you, too, are staying." Looking at me as if I shared Foster's guilt.

"I had the choice of three hotels here which are allowed to take Blacks," I told him.

"Yes, I know," he interrupted.

"Let me explain. I was told this at the airport the moment I arrived. I was told that there were no other hotels I could go to, none owned by Blacks or Indians or Coloreds or anyone else other than Whites. I make no apology for staying there."

"Okay. Okay. I accept that you had no choice, but people like you and Foster and Ashe are setting back the black struggle ten years. By coming here. By letting South Africa use the fact of your coming to counter our accusations of discrimination."

It finally got through to me that he had invited me to see him, not really to tell me about Robben Island, though he answered my questions, but to protest my visit to his country. He'd mentioned that he'd tried to reach both Foster and Ashe without any success.

"How do you imagine anyone outside your country would know anything about conditions here if no one made any attempt to learn at first hand?" I asked.

"You could learn without coming here. Especially

you. You were at the United Nations. Didn't you meet any of our brothers who went there to petition? Some of our brothers from here and South West Africa made it over to the States. Didn't any of them see you?"

"Yes. I met some of them."

"Didn't you believe what they told you?"

"I was persuaded by what they told me."

"Don't give me all that diplomatic shit, man. Either you believed them or you didn't."

"I was generally persuaded by them, but I welcomed the opportunity to see the situation for myself. This is it."

"Do you dash off to every country to check everything for yourself?"

"No."

"Then why this? Did you have any difficulty getting a visa from this government?"

"No."

"Shit, man, doesn't that tell you anything? Your books were banned in this country. Even today Blacks can't see your film in the public bijou, and that, too, was banned to Whites for some time. In spite of all that these Afrikaners gave you a visa to come here. Think, man! Can't you see they're planning to use you?"

"Look, they can plan what the hell they like, that has nothing to do with me. I was issued a visa. Fine. But nobody can control how I think about what I see and hear and feel." And, on impulse added, "Not even you."

He laughed, reaching forward to touch me.

"You think so? You really think so? By the time these sons-of-bitches are through with you, you'll be singing their tune without realizing it. You'll go back to the States and tell people all about how freely you were allowed to move about. No supervision, therefore, no police state.

Which makes a liar out of all of us. Right? They'll wine you and dine you and prove that educated Blacks can make it anywhere. Only the lazy Bantu has to be kicked in the ass and locked in a ghetto to make him stir himself. They'll forget to tell you that he is disenfranchised, denied a reasonable education and the right to bargain for his labor and compete for the job he wants to do. Yes, friend, they'll tell you you're different and, you know something, you'll end up believing it."

"Think what you like," I said.

"Eh?"

"Think what the hell you like," I repeated and stood up to leave. "Look, you invited me and I came to talk with you. I thought you'd tell me about what the life is like for you and others. I came because I wanted to learn the truth, to hear it for myself so I can write about it. I expected that you, black like me, would lay it on me, without all this bullshit. You think I was born yesterday? I've lived most of my adult life among Whites. London, Paris, New York, Rome. I've no illusions about them, but I don't see them as bloody supermen either. They can't control how I think and what I'll write." He had needled me to this point. He and the others. Who the hell did they think they were? Pouring their suspicions over me. Here they were locked tight in the rotten ghetto and wanting the outside world to know of their plight. Okay. I'd come in. Of my own free will. So tell me and I'll write it. That's what I was saying to them, but all I was getting was their suspicion and scorn.

"Hey, cool it, man." He reached forward and pushed me back into the chair. "Don't get excited. We're talking. Relax."

"You relax. You call that talking, making me seem like some half-assed idiot just because I've visited your country?

White newsmen and writers fly here regularly, write their pieces and fly out again. Do you warn them that they're being used?"

"Fuck them."

"And fuck you, too, mate. What gives you the right to be so high and mighty? Your years on Robben Island? Okay, I sympathize."

"Stuff your sympathy. Hell, man, you're beginning to sound like Whitey. Cool down. I'm only trying to help you. And don't hand me that shit about Paris and London. Over there they might hate your guts, but the law limits what they can do to you. Here Whitey *is* the law. Blacks can't command the law because it was not intended for them. They can't demand justice, because it was not intended for them. Justice and the law are concepts which apply to men. To humans. In this society Blacks are not considered human so they are not sheltered by those concepts. Did you know that, in this society we have no vote? We're not even on the official census. Shit man, we're not here. Don't talk to me about Whites in Europe or America. These here are different. They're fascists of the worst kind.

"Look," he was leaning forward, tapping on my knee with a long finger. "All I'm begging you to do is think. I'm black. You're black. I published a few newsletters which nobody outside this town ever heard of and they threw me into jail. You've written books which have been read by millions. Attacking the very policies they live by. Okay, they try to keep those books out, but they're brought in anyway and read, so to save their own fucking face, they lift the ban. That makes this a liberal society. Right? And to cap it all, they let you in. Man, they used you before you stepped into that airplane."

The logic of it hit me hard, killing my anger and stirring up the fears I'd earlier had about making the visit.

The visa was five months in coming. Perhaps all that time was necessary while the design was worked out. Christ, I was beginning to think like him.

"Okay, you made your point. Now I must be running along. I've a few things to do." I wanted to be out of this.

"Like a dinner engagement, maybe? With some of your white friends?" Grinning.

"Perhaps." He had the knack of finding the nerve.

"Don't worry. They've enough black slaves to keep it hot for you. Okay, man. Like you say, you can see and hear and think for yourself, but I tell you they'll use you. They do it all the time. Among us. Even out there on the Island. Can you imagine that? Even out there where you'd think we were all brothers, all there for the same reason, all united against the fascist bastards. Even there they managed to use some of us against others. And for what? Some fucking little privilege we'd already learned to live without. After all we'd been through, to sell one's soul for shit like that! So you see man, telling me that you can see and hear and think for yourself doesn't mean a damn thing. Anyway, while you're thinking for yourself, think about us and remember that in the eyes of these fascists you're no better than the rest of us."

"I'll remember," I said. I'd come to this house with a gutful of goodwill toward this man. Now all I could feel was a nagging suspicion that somehow I'd been trapped into betraying him and others like him. Just by being in their country.

"In prison the payoff was some worthless little privilege," he was still with it. "What are they giving you? The 'Honorary White' bit, so you can believe yourself different from the rest of us? Fancy hotel, your face in the white newspaper, moving around freely? Same thing, man. Privileges bought—"

"Nobody's bought me," I said, lamely.

"—And paid for, man. And when you think you're moving about more freely than the rest of us, just look over your shoulder. If you're quick enough you might learn something."

Everything he said struck home. Sure, I had been telling myself that nobody was restricting or supervising my movements. I'd been in and out of Soweto and Alexandra, hadn't I? My only problem had been my inability to make contact with the so-called black representatives. Buthelezi. Matanzima. The Information Office had promised me meetings with them but had only come up with excuses. Always at the last moment. But I must not let the things this man was saying color everything that happened. If I couldn't reach the big Blacks, there would be others.

"Are you concerned for me or just sorry for yourself?" I asked, trying to throw him on the defensive, and free myself from the suffocation of his penetrating insight.

"I'm not sorry for me, man. I'll live. I lost ten years of my life out there on the island. Doing shit, man. Breaking rocks for the sake of breaking rocks. You're sitting on a pile of rocks today with a hammer in your hand and sometime next week or the week after it's a pile of pebbles and you can't remember how it happened. You've used two weeks of your life watching rocks turn to dust. And the next week you're sitting on another pile of rocks. Or is it the same one? You know what they did with the pebbles, man? They just left them there to remind us that we were just shit. You know what our ambition was? To stay alive. Staying alive, that's all. Living for news from outside. Do you know what was the most important thing to us in there? Not money, man. Not pussy. A newspaper. Any old newspaper. We read every word. Everything. And we talked. Can you understand? Those fucking Afrikaner guards watched us to prevent us from talking. Threatened us. Punished us. But we talked. Even with our mouths shut like, what you call them, ventriloquists, man. Whoever found a piece of newspaper read it, then passed it on and told everyone what he'd read. After a while we were reading more closely, more perceptively than when we were free. We shared our points of view. We talked. Especially about the political situation." Here he laughed again, scratching his head, remembering.

"Once a priest came into the prison carrying a briefcase with a newspaper, the *Times*, stuck under the flap. Like lightning, it disappeared. He never made a fuss about it. That Sunday we had a whole newspaper to read. After that, whenever that priest came to see us, he brought a newspaper and it always disappeared from his briefcase. Survival, man, that's the word. Nelson Mandela is up there. Living it out from hour to hour. That's where you learn about hope, man. Without it you're dead."

He came and placed a hand on my arm, a conciliatory gesture.

"Will you come and see me again, friend? I promise to be nice."

"Don't strain yourself on my account."

"That's not a strain. Living like this is a strain. Shit, I can't even see you to the door. Never know who might be checking on me from outside. If I'm seen talking to you, they could come and take me away. Fucking lovely way to live, isn't it? I'm jealous, man. You, a stranger, can move about as you wish. Right? Me, a native son, I'm denied the right to step outside. Goodnight, man."

I left him, his words continuing their disturbing refrain in my ear. I'd gone to his house to talk with him about his time in prison. He'd talked about my visit to his country, sowing in my mind a very sizable seed of doubt about my own motives, and my possible malleability by the South African authorities. Walking away from the Indian's irritating sneers, I wondered if he was right.

He'd questioned my coming to South Africa but he'd either forgotten or ignored the fact that my coming made it possible for me to see him and hear his cynical censure. In his position, I'd be just as embittered, seeing strangers move about with ease while I was restricted to my own house. But what the hell did he want of me?

5

On my way back to the hotel, I passed a restaurant, brightly lit and attractive, and suddenly realizing I was hungry, I decided to go in. I pushed the door but got no further than a step inside, where I was confronted by a waiter, dead-faced and stony-eyed, who placed himself in front of me. He said something to me which I supposed was in Afrikaans.

"What did you say?" I asked.

"You do not come in." This was stupid. I was already in and thinking out my next move. Now I fully realized why the hotel people had repeatedly suggested that I let them know whenever I wanted to dine out and they would make the arrangements for me, claiming that they knew where all the best eating places were located. This waiter looked as if he would have welcomed a fracas, eyes pale, pugnacious jaw thrust forward. I was turning to leave when another man approached and asked him something in Afrikaans. The waiter replied, and the newcomer then addressed me.

"I don't speak your language," I said.

"You're not African?"

"No, I'm a visitor." At which he spoke again to the pale-eyed waiter, this time impatiently, but I walked out, wishing them both to whatever hell was reserved for Afrikaners.

In my room, the things the Indian had said teased and tormented me, throwing into sharp relief what had happened at the restaurant. The waiter's contempt for Blacks was ready and waiting for expression. A waiter! His awkward English indicated that he may well have been a foreigner, an immigrant. How quickly people took on the local social coloration. Like chameleons. Come to think of it I hadn't seen a restaurant in Soweto or Alexandra. Maybe I passed them and didn't notice. What were they like? Could I eat a meal in one of them? Christ!

My reflections were interrupted by a telephone call from a young black newsman I'd met a few days earlier.

"How are you doing?"

"Fine," I lied.

"How would you like to come out here and see how some of us live?"

"Where's 'out here'?"

"Soweto."

"I've been there."

"Soweto's a big place. I don't think you'd have come to this part. I heard you'd visited with the big boys here. Come and see how the little people live."

Safely indoors, I wasn't keen to go out again. Besides, I'd had enough of social exposure for one night. A quick tray from room service seemed a more attractive alternative.

"How could I get there now," I temporized. "It's nearly eight o'clock."

"By taxi. Black taxi. No white taxi will bring you out here. Get a black taxi from the taxi stand near the black bus stop. I'll meet you at this end. It will do you good to travel the way the rest of us do." I was still far from enthusiastic.

"How will I get back here?" I asked, thinking of the special permit required of Blacks in the city at night.

"I'll see to it, don't worry about that."

"Okay," I surrendered and went out to the black bus stop across the park. I was directed to a taxi, empty while the driver stood around joking with friends. Loud laughter punctuated each sally. He waved me to sit inside. Soon I was joined by another passenger who sat beside me without saying a word. Then another and another, followed by two more, these sitting in the front. Not a word from anyone. Another person pushed in the back and we were all forced to sit diagonally pressed together. Another passenger slipped into the front. A woman. At first I thought she'd be driving because she sat at the wheel, but now the driver got in, pushing against the woman until he could take hold of the wheel even though his body was only halfway under it. Somehow he started the vehicle and we were off.

It was the most uncomfortable taxi ride I'd ever taken. Eight adults cramped uncomfortably into space designed for five, the driver miraculously shifting gears and steering from his sideways position. We passed several taxis similarly overloaded, always with Blacks.

In Soweto, my acquaintance was waiting as promised, standing beside his car. He said he could have fetched me, but thought the experience of riding as he did twice each day would help me to understand better what was normal for a Black. He kept his car for after-work use.

We drove to his home, one of the square concrete box-like structures in the northeast part of Soweto. Instead of the corrugated metal roof I'd seen on some of the other houses, this one and its neighbors wore bulky concrete tops, making them seem humpbacked in the nighttime gloom, very much, in fact, like huge sleeping elephants. Inside it was hot, even with the few windows open. Several candles were strategically placed about the room for light. Indoors he turned to me and said, "Welcome to the real Soweto."

The house was sparsely furnished. The main room in which I stood contained a wooden table with three wooden chairs around it, a rough chest of drawers reaching nearly to the low ceiling, and a narrow wooden cot. In a corner another table, roughly made but sturdy, supported some cooking utensils and a Primus stove. No electricity. No signs of running water.

"Six of us live here, in four little rooms," he said, his eyes brightly on me as if to note my slightest reaction. He led me into another room which was furnished in nearly the same way, except that there was no cooking equipment. A central wooden table, two low cots opposite each other and two wooden cupboards. Near one of the cots was a small upended box, centrally divided, which contained several books. Crowning the box was a half-worn candle stuck in a Coke bottle.

"My brother is a medical student, one of the very few. That's where he studies. He leaves here at five o'clock each morning to make his way into town and compete with white boys who read by electric light, sleep in comfortable beds and eat a good breakfast." Saying it all so matter-of-factly. I looked at him and surprised the pain on his face.

"Different from your hotel, don't you think?" he asked.

"Yes, different."

"Different from those houses they showed you on your officially conducted tour, I'm sure. Then, you saw houses like this, but with electric lighting and a kitchen sink and a water toilet out back. I'm sure they didn't show you these.

How would you like to live here for a month? No, a week, or even a day?"

I was feeling battered, first by the Indian, then that bastard at the restaurant, now this. How much crap was I supposed to take? I wanted to see, at first hand, the conditions under which my fellow Blacks lived, but why should they think they had a right to cram it down my throat?

"I wouldn't wish to live here," I replied. Leaving it at that.

"How about a drink?" he asked, not waiting for my response, but reaching into a cupboard for two china mugs and a tin of powdered coffee. He poured water from a container into a tin kettle, then set to pumping away at the Primus stove, pricking at the jet from time to time and cursing under his breath as it defied his efforts.

"Not to worry," I said, actually relieved that the little stove was defiant. After all he'd said I wasn't too anxious to risk the water, even though it would of course be boiled. Wondering if he had to go through this same exercise early every morning to have hot water for shaving. What happened in the winter? Apart from the bare necessities there was nothing. No curtains, no posters, no pictures.

The failure of the coffee project seemed to cause us both some embarrassment, but he saved the situation by inviting me to take a walk around the neighborhood. Outside the night was star-studded and pleasantly warm, the night shadows smudging the outlines of bush, tree, and house, giving the whole place a romantic softness. No street lamp in this part of town, only the candleshine from open doorways and the starlight from above.

"It's okay if we walk around here together at night," he told me, "but any one of us alone would be asking for trouble. You call it mugging in the United States. Bands of young boys roam the streets at night, preying on men who've been drinking in the local beer gardens or in the shebeens. Beat them up and rob them. Sometimes kill them. Know how they do it? They push a piece of sharpened wire, something like a short knitting needle, into the neck at the base of the skull. Paralyzes those who survive. Many of the paraplegics in the local hospital are victims of the Tsotsis."

"Why do you call them that? What does it mean?"

"Not too sure. Something to do with the Zoot Suit gangs of the United States, I've heard. Anyway, so the story goes. Most of them are boys without parents or even relatives. School dropouts. Or maybe they couldn't get into school. Couldn't afford the fees, or clothes, or books. So they don't go. After all, schooling is compulsory only for Whites. Optional for Blacks."

We walked around, listening to the night sounds, people talking to each other, snatches of conversation floating out from the houses, all in an African dialect. Music. Edmundo Ros swinging his inimitable way through a rumba rebroadcast from London. The sudden scream of a night bird in the near distance. We could have been light years away from the neat, trim suburbs designated "White." In order to reach this place from my hotel the route had been through suburb after suburb of affluence and comfort. My companion and hundreds of thousands like him made the same trip to and fro each day, seeing the affluence, envying the comfort. Inevitably hating.

"I think I should be heading back to town." I said.

"Had enough?"

I told him it wasn't that. I was anxious about being stopped by the police. If that happened and they found out that I was a visitor they'd also discover that I had no permit to be in Soweto.

"Nobody's going to stop us. Not unless there's a police raid to find people illegally living here."

"Do you know when a raid is likely to happen?"

"No."

"Then I'd better get back."

Hoping he'd see the point and agree. Realizing, belatedly, that I was completely dependent on him now for leaving that place. There were no telephone booths to be seen, no taxi stands, no bus stops. If there were any such places, only he knew where they were.

Now and then a car passed us, always hurrying. No pedestrians. Perhaps the Tsotsis keep nighttime walking to a minimum. Abruptly he turned and we retraced our steps to his house where we got into his car and headed out of Soweto.

"The trick is not to have a breakdown at night," he said. "No help for the black motorist, not even from the police. If you have a breakdown and a policeman approaches you, the first thing he asks is not what's wrong with the car, no, he wants to see your pass."

We made it without incident to my hotel where he left me and hurried off home. I wished him a safe journey, asking myself if the trips, his and mine, were worth the risk and anxiety. I could so easily have jeopardized the rest of my stay. I promised myself I'd not do it again.

I sat and thought over the events of the day which had been painful and very irritating. Here I was a black stranger in this country and it was becoming more and more difficult to meet and consort with Blacks without being subject to suspicious inquiry. Inside me, I felt deep identification with them in their unhappy state. Everything I'd seen and heard since entering the country merely strengthened that feeling, because I knew that the only thing which saved me from the same fate was the fact that I was a national of another sovereign state. I wouldn't want to live as they lived, but neither did they. I was prepared to be with them whenever they wished, to learn from them, about them. I didn't wait for them to seek me out. I sought them. But evidently that was not enough. Okay, so they thought I'd be used by their Government. I believed them to be wrong. So why couldn't they give me the benefit of the doubt? I was already in the country. If I looked and listened and heard and then went off and wrote laudatory pieces in spite of all the evidence to the contrary, then they could call me traitor.

White journalists I'd met in London and New York had given me the impression that they'd been able to talk with Blacks in South Africa without much difficulty. If that were true why were these Blacks making things so difficult for me? So different from my visits to other parts of Africa, where I'd been made to feel welcome. Immediately. My black skin was my ticket to enter. Here, it was the reverse; my very blackness was the barrier. Well, perhaps I should be patient. After all, the conditions I'd already seen were worse than I'd dreamed possible and those very conditions might be the reasons for my black friends' suspicions and reservations.

The hotel's public relations officer telephoned and said she hoped that all was well with me.

"If there's any way in which I can be of help to you, please don't hesitate to ask," she said.

"Right now, all I ask of life is a hot bath, a cold drink and a funny movie," I replied, lightheartedly.

"The bath and drink are no problem," she told me, "but the movie is another matter. If you're really keen to go to the bijou, though, and decide what you want to see, I could telephone the management and I'm sure it could be arranged."

"Why telephone? I don't understand."

"I think I'd better come up to your suite and explain,"

she said. A few minutes later, she arrived, blonde and well-groomed, with that quiet confidence which seems to be the stock-in-trade of the public relations fraternity.

Seated, she said, "I think I must explain the bijou situation here in South Africa. Most cinemas are operated for Whites only. We call them bijous here. There are a few for Coloreds and Blacks in their own areas. Indians have their own. In any case, those in Johannesburg are for Whites only. As an important visitor to our country you are allowed, shall we say, special status. I feel sure that if you decide on the film you want to see, I can telephone the management and there will be no difficulty."

"You mean I couldn't just go to the box office and buy a ticket?"

"Not unless they're expecting you. It's the law, I'm afraid." It suddenly struck me that in this country I could not, for an hour or two, lose myself in the temporary anonymity of a darkened cinema the way I'd done in every other country in which I'd lived or visited. It had been a favorite way of slipping away from pressing reality, a painless, absorbing way of insuring the quick passage of time. A thought occurred to me.

"What happened when the film *To Sir, with Love* was shown here?"

"Same thing."

"No Blacks allowed to see the black actor?"

"Not here in Johannesburg. Blacks and Whites are prohibited by law from congregating in the same place. Anyway, they wouldn't have missed much, because the film was so badly censored it was difficult to follow the sequence of events. Anything between the black teacher and the white one, Gillian, was cut out. I know, because I saw it first at the bijou and then I saw the whole movie at a private showing in a friend's house. It's possible to rent an uncut film from one of the rental agencies. Anybody can rent them, Black or White, as long as they have the money."

"So if I wanted to see a movie, I'd have to pay for my ticket then beg permission to get in, right?"

"Well, I wouldn't put it quite like that. We at this hotel would do whatever we could to avoid any embarrassment to you."

I thanked her and, soon after, she left. I had no quarrel with her. I thought of walking off my irritation in the streets, but then remembered my near encounter with the policeman. The only alternative was a bath, a cold beer, and settling down with pencil and paper to review the days already passed in this beautiful city, this very uncomfortable society.

Some days later, early in the morning, a group of black welfare officers came to the hotel asking to see me. I invited them up to my room, wondering how the word of my presence had got around.

There were five of them, two women and three men, all of them employed to service one or other area of welfare for Blacks. They complained of the inadequacies of the service and reminded me that I had been involved in nearly similar situations as recorded in my book *Paid Servant*, which they had read. They could not begin to cope with even a tiny part of the problems people brought to them, and they wondered if I could offer them any advice. Listening, I learned that ten of them were expected to service Soweto and Alexandra, a total population of well over a million people. Their office was in white Johannesburg, and both the limited programs undertaken and the minimal funds available were subject to white control. The biggest problem was the many dislocated, neglected children who roamed the streets of the townships living on what they could beg or steal, homeless, without parents or relatives. According to the supervising authorities these children were not legally of the townships and therefore did not qualify for any official assistance. They could not go to school even if they wanted to because a new law required all legitimate parent-residents to have a pink school card for their child. Without it no child was accepted as a pupil.

White children, if neglected or abandoned, are cared for at Government expense. They would in no circumstances be allowed to wander about like homeless dogs eating garbage. I told them that I had seen an elderly white woman throwing chunks of bread to the pigeons and how, as soon as she'd wandered away, the children drove the pigeons off and collected the bread, eating it hungrily. Oddly I saw none of them begging.

The white welfare officers were the bosses and called the tune. Colored officers dealt with colored clients, Asian officers with Asian clients, black officers with Blacks. Levels of payment differed for each officer group. It became apparent that they were their own most needy clients, their own welfare their most pressing priority.

We talked for most of the morning, taking a short break for coffee which I ordered. There was something a little bizarre about us. In the park outside were living reminders of the urgency of their work, yet they sounded so much like welfare workers I've known in England, France, and the United States. The same pompous preoccupation with the jargon of their profession, the same insistence on separating themselves in every way from their "clients." They emphasized that they were trained and qualified as sociologists, forgetting their earlier complaint that Blacks are denied access to anything more than the median levels of qualification.

From time to time, the door to my suite would be

opened and one of the floor supervisors, white, would peer at us from the vestibule and quickly retreat with a "Sorry, just checking to see that everything's okay." I assumed that it was just the normal hotel practice. It has happened to me in many parts of the world. My visitors, however, felt quite differently. They believed that we were being watched and that the interruptions would continue as long as they remained with me.

"They think we're plotting something up here," one of the women said.

"Blacks talking together are always supposed to be plotting. To kill them or steal from them. That's why that one comes in without knocking."

"What's surprising about that?" from another. "We're watched, and I'm sure our American friend is being watched. Wouldn't surprise me if these rooms are bugged." Suddenly getting up to peer among the artificial plants, behind the sofas, under the tables. Everywhere.

"Why worry?" I asked, smiling. "We've not been plotting, so who cares if someone's listening to us? Surely it should come as no surprise to anyone to hear that black children are homeless and starving."

"Survival, friend, survival. Mustn't make anything too easy for them. You probably think we've been reading too many spy novels. In this place you say something out of line and they have you hanging, like a fish. You're lucky you can afford to be amused at us."

"I'm not amused at you." Christ, would I never escape having to defend myself.

"Stay here six months, or three months, and you'll understand what we're talking about."

On this subdued note, they left me.

The meeting with the Bantu Council had been arranged for eight o'clock that evening in the home of one of the members. I would have preferred to meet them in the Council building where I could see them against their working background but naturally I was obliged to follow their arrangements.

One of them called for me promptly at seven o'clock. On the way to Soweto, I told him of my earlier visit with the white guide and the old man's outburst which had led to this meeting. He seemed preoccupied, glancing in the rear-view mirror more often than I thought necessary, and I was surprised when he suddenly asked, "Is anyone following you?"

I didn't know how to respond to that. "Why?" I asked.

"Just trying to make sure," he replied, and said no more about it. On arrival at his home, his wife greeted us with the news that two members of the Security Police, one black and one white, had been there asking about me and the meeting, claiming that they wanted to make sure I would be quite safe. She replied that I would be under their roof, as safe as they were, as protected as they were, if any protection was necessary. They replied that it was their duty to prevent an international incident and merely wanted assurance that all would be well.

"I gave them short shrift," she said, smiling.

This was my first experience of the Security Police actually monitoring my movements. It was no longer a joke, an offshoot of my friend's paranoia, but undeniable proof of the Big Brother interest in my movements. My hosts seemed to take it all in stride. They told me that police spying was merely another fact of daily life; it pervaded every area of living to the point where no one fully trusted his neighbor or associates or friends. This was equally true of the Council: although they were all black, each one was afraid that another might report something said or done in the hope of receiving some minuscule concession from the Security Police.

"That way they keep us distrustful of each other, suspicious, so we're unwilling to come together in any real way to help each other. If I have a new idea, I don't know where to start. I can discuss it with my wife, but who else? Sometimes people come to me with ideas. I've got to listen very carefully. If their ideas have the slightest hint of opposition to Government policy, my first reaction is that they're trying to trap me. Oh, yes, that's part of the technique. They come to you with an idea and the next thing you know they claim it was your idea in the first place and you have the Security Police on your back. All the time the police hold over your head the threat of sending you off to one of the Homelands. They could come here tomorrow and claim I'd been instigating something and deport me out of here. They'd tell me to remove my house from the Government's land. How do I go about picking up a house like this? They've got us Blacks in a vise. As a result we don't trust each other. We talk, sure, we talk, but we watch what we say. So, now you know. We'll meet here tonight with you and we'll tell you some things you could hear from anyone else. That's safe. But wait till you ask us questions that require us to express our deep feelings, questions that get to the bone. Then see what happens. We begin to look at each other. My friend, the Whites have got us so that each one of us has become the other's policeman."

"Then this exercise tonight is likely to be a waste of time," I suggested.

"Not altogether. Wait and see for yourself." But I was right.

By eight o'clock no one else had arrived. At eight thirty-five one showed up bringing his wife and a friend as if it were a party. Ten minutes later another arrived, with his wife and a local schoolmaster. No sign of the aggressive little councillor whose challenge to me had precipitated the whole thing. I asked my host about him and learned that he had been informed of the meeting and had promised to attend. By nine fifteen, he had still not come and someone left to fetch him but soon came back saying that he was not at home.

"After his little performance at the Council Office in front of the white woman guide, someone's had a word with him, I suppose," one of the men suggested.

I was surprised to learn that everyone knew of the incident, insignificant though it had seemed to me.

Three young men showed up, none of them councillors, one of them a newsman working for a city newspaper. Conversation settled on the safe topic of the schools. The schoolmaster was praised on all sides for the wonderful job he was doing, even though it emerged that the children's big successes were in their competitive singing, rather than in their academic work. Of the six to seven hours of the school day, at least two hours were spent rehearsing songs, mostly European songs.

Discreet questioning disclosed that the schools in Soweto are poorly equipped, the teachers poorly trained, the pupils ill-prepared to compete in the harshly competitive society; and here were these black men congratulating each other. When I probed further on the schools, on teacher and pupil performance, they readily resorted to a lengthy litany of woes, all of which were blamed on the Government and so outside their control.

I was soon bored with it all. I had been led to believe that they were ready and able to talk freely with me about their community, but all that had taken place were moans, evasions, and backslapping. What the hell had they to be proud of? The few schools they had were overcrowded, understaffed, and ill-equipped. Large numbers of children were roaming the streets instead of being in school, and the devilish "pink card" system kept it so. More and more of these children were pressured into Tsotsi gangs, and these men, each secure in his own circumscribed job, did nothing to change the situation.

I stood up to leave, just as the hostess brought a tray of drinks on which the other guests avidly fell as if that were the real reason for the gathering. If real change would come to places like Soweto, it would not be through the efforts of men such as these, I realized.

On the way to my hotel, my host and I said little, each wrapped in his own assessment of the abortive meeting. Now and then he slowed down to allow another car to pass us, and I realized he was still afraid that I was being followed. Or perhaps he was concerned for himself. So easily one could be caught in the grip of paranoia.

Lying on my bed, reviewing the day's events, I was disturbed by the non-appearance of the little Soweto councillor. I had been told that he knew I would be there to see him. After his spirited effort in front of my white guide, he would want to be there, as face-saving is very important among people. I wondered if she had complained to her superiors about his outburst and a decision had been made to silence him, at least for the duration of my stay. With all that I heard about the police and their tactics, he had invited a pack of trouble for himself. But perhaps it was worth it, to him. Perhaps he had reviewed his life and had seized the opportunity to make a gesture, to himself. In the prevailing circumstances, that small gesture assumed heroic proportions. No other Black had said or done as much. Not publicly. Not in the presence of a member of white official-dom.

6

The next day was the day of the promised lunch at the Afrikaner businessmen's club arranged by the banker I had met at Helen Suzman's. On the way there he explained the growth and development of the white community.

A man eminently knowledgeable about money, its power and influence, he spoke easily of his plans for the future. He spoke of the club to which we were going, its founding and the type of people who were its members. He warned that I might find them inflexible in their social attitudes, but hoped I'd be patient and remember that they were the products of a grim period in South Africa's history when men and women needed to fight for the land on which to settle and establish communities. For my benefit, he recounted the Afrikaner version of those wars of conquest, stressing the courage and fortitude of the voortrekkers and their womenfolk. He spoke of the bloody conflicts in which Afrikaners of earlier generations had frequently been involved and made it seem that they had invariably been on the defensive against a persistent, devious, and intractable enemy. Memory dies hard and I got the impression that Afrikaner hatred of Blacks is deliberately kept alive today, primarily for tactical political purposes. I reminded him that the wars of which he spoke were several generations old. Since then the whole world had been torn by wars far graver than those the voortrekkers fought and yet had shown a willingness to rise above the hates and fears which had given rise to those crises. What was there so special about South Africa that it needed to "feed fat its ancient grudge"?

It is both distressing and fascinating to hear people defend their contempt and hatred of Blacks, especially to me, a man as black or blacker than their enemy. I asked him if he and his kind had no concern for the inevitable bloody results if they persisted in their despotic pressure of the Blacks.

At this, his tune changed. He denied contempt, citing his own friendly relationship with the Blacks he employed on his farm.

"I'm willing to admit that changes must come," he said. "They will come. But we must not expect them overnight. We can't have revolution here. Evolution yes, but not revolution." The words flowing so easily from him, cushioned in comfort as he was by the blood, sweat, and toil of the Blacks whom he despised. He could talk of evolution, secure behind the vast stockpiles of armaments and the military manpower deployed strategically all over the country—I pulled myself up short. I was on my way to hear from him and others like him, so the thing to do was wait and listen to them.

The Clubhouse was much as I expected, an attractive red-brick building set against a pleasant background of carefully nurtured trees and trimmed lawns and flower beds. Beginning at the doorway, uniformed servants everywhere, all black, ready to dart off at the master's bidding, all eyeing me with surprise and speculation, the first black person ever to set foot in that building in other than a menial capacity.

Settled in the well-appointed lounge with my host to await the other guests, I drank a glass of sherry with him, amused that we were in fact breaking the law which forbade Blacks and Whites to drink alcoholic beverages together. Unable to keep the thought to myself, I shared it with him.

"Let's put it this way," he told me. "You're an overseas visitor, a world famous author, VIP. During your stay in South Africa you have the honorary status of a white man."

That spoiled it for me, my mood of friendly ease evaporating completely, giving way to a rage which I fought to control. I put my glass down and looked at him, hating the arrogance which led him to assume that he, they, could change the color of my skin to suit their whim. No, not change it. Just overlook it, ignore it to the point where it did not exist for them and they could superimpose their choice upon it. But no, just looking at them convinced me that my blackness was there before them, large and unavoidable; it was plain from the way they behaved when we were introduced—the hurried pleased-to-meet-you, the words rushed out to belie their meaning; the quick retreat from my deliberately firm handshake.

I had half expected to meet a group of highly intelligent, urbane men, as conversant with world affairs as they were knowledgeable about their particular interests, articulate and arrogantly relaxed in the assurance of their power and prestige. Instead, I found myself in a group of rather ordinary people, most of them painfully hesitant on matters outside their parochial concerns and generally uncomfortable in the unfamiliar company of a black man who did not treat them as his betters.

Two of them, an elderly economist and a physicist,

seemed more relaxed than the rest, and keen to discuss South Africa's international image, even though they took a lofty view of the criticism directed at her. They argued that the continuing international economic crises were working to South Africa's advantage, and would eventually have the effect of forcing some accommodation to her domestic policies. In support of this, they pointed to their country's considerable gold reserves, the rapid rise in the price of gold, and the new political leverage which, they claimed, South Africa could now exercise.

"In this world, money talks," the economist said, "and the loudest, most persuasive voice is that of gold. Even some African countries which publicly criticize us because of our domestic policies are willing to make private economic agreements with us. Out of such agreements political accommodations are born."

So we drank and talked, watched covertly by the black serving team which quietly and efficiently attended us. I wondered how they viewed my presence among the white men. Did they too assume that I was being used by the Whites? I could read nothing behind their unsmiling faces and courteous manner.

Then lunch was ready and we were seated, and I realized that this was a first for all or nearly all of them. They were sharing the same board on equal terms with a black man, and no matter how they might rationalize it to themselves that simple fact was incontrovertible. There was the usual friendly chitchat as each tried to settle down. I wondered how each would report this meeting to wife, children, and business associates. And what would they tell the Blacks who serve them at home and with whom they claimed to have good personal relationships?

I remembered chatting in a park a few days before with a maid who was supervising a small white child and a dog. I tried to question her about social conditions in South Africa, but, inevitably, she brought up Bob Foster.

"How he beat that white man! It was so good."

Her whole body glowed with the sharing in that small victory, this woman whose life was destined to be spent in lowly service, nurturing the children who would one day grow up to treat her with casual contempt, whether it was personal or public. She would be used, underpaid, kept in her place . . .

Now here were these men, most of whom had in their time been bathed and comforted by black women, casually defending their inhuman policies with the spurious claim of "good relationships." Spurious? They were completely sincere and convinced of their righteousness.

After lunch, I was formally introduced to the group and invited to address them. On the spur of the moment I decided to talk on the economics of waste, deliberately choosing that neutral approach to tease them out of their shells, to let them feel comfortable with the Honorary White and open up so that I might learn about them. I said that I had been impressed by Johannesburg and its flourishing suburbs, but sickened by the wide evidence of the exclusion of Blacks from the essential life of the community. Blacks were everywhere, cleaning, serving, providing an inescapably solid base to the community's economic life, but resentfully, unwillingly, because they were denied the right to exercise their imaginative potential. I asked them to explain how a community could ever reach its full growth if the greater part of its people were restricted to minimal contribution. As I saw it the result was waste on an unbelievable scale, shrouded behind the absurdities of discrimination.

They listened in silence but when I sat down they defended themselves vociferously. They insisted that the

Blacks of South Africa are better off economically than Blacks in any other part of Africa. They told me that though there was job reservation which favored Whites, the law required every man to be paid the rate for the job, and that those employers guilty of evading that law were invariably foreign firms, particularly American.

They insisted that I had not been in the country long enough to see and understand the complexities of the labor structure in general, nor the conditions affecting the black role in particular. Very few Blacks, they claimed, were capable of other than menial employment. South African Blacks had changed little from their original primitive state and were, for the most part, still happier living in the rural Homelands in their traditional way. On the other hand, the grim conditions in which the black workers lived were not really intolerable to them, being an improvement on what they knew in their familiar rural living. It was Communists and outside agitators who stirred them up and tried to make them dissatisfied with their lot. Rural Blacks were discouraged from taking their families with them to the urban centers only because that would have meant too great a dislocation, in addition to the aggravated problems of housing, feeding, and educating their children. On and on. The old familiar clichés, but trotted out with the utmost sincerity. As I listened it was difficult for me to keep my mounting irritation under control. I am as black as the men and women they were talking about.

But I was a stranger. I would be here today and gone tomorrow. I needed nothing from them, so they could afford to be generous with their time and their rhetoric. Perhaps they expected me to be flattered by being among them, treated as an equal by them. Nudged by the irritation which would not subside I said, "I understand you've broken the 'Afrikaner Only' rule in this club and admitted

Englishmen. That tells me you're getting around to forgiving and forgetting what Kitchener and his redcoats did during the Boer War." There was silence for a few moments, not even the tinkle of ice in a glass. Then someone said:

"We've come a long way since those days. Language aside, we're all South Africans here."

"That's what I was thinking," I said. "Maybe the same spirit will foster a similarly reasonable attitude to the Zulu Wars and the descendants of those who fought in them."

Silence.

"Here am I," I went on, "sitting with you. I have no way of knowing where my ancestors came from. History suggests that nowhere in Africa was secure from the slaver's nets."

They were watching me, most faces wearing that pained half-smile which was as much as courtesy demanded.

"What's your point, Mr. Braithwaite?" one asked.

"I'm anticipating the day when Blacks might be admitted to membership of your club. After all, one ex-enemy is as good as another. You could always designate them Honorary White." My little quip fell flat. Even the half-smiles had vanished.

"The designation Honorary White is merely a convenience reserved for overseas visitors," one said. "We do not wish to embarrass them by any regulations designed specifically to deal with domestic circumstances."

"Yes. I know," I replied, turning the needle. "Yesterday, some men I met in a park near my hotel mistook me for a Zulu, so I must look like one. I'm merely considering the possibility that I might be descended from one."

7

My next plan was to visit the Transkei, one of the Government-designated "Homeland" areas. It was an hour's plane ride from Johannesburg to Durban, the nearest airport to the Transkei. A car with a driver awaited me at the airport and we immediately took off on the three-hundred-fifty-mile road journey to Umtata, the capital town of the Transkei. I had expected that here, in a predominantly black enclave which was supposedly preparing itself for independence, I would find Blacks in control in all departments and at all levels of political, social, and economic life. My eyes were soon opened. At the Information Office, my first stop, the staff were all Afrikaners, officials of the central Government. The Information Officer welcomed me and promised to arrange for me to tour the Transkei. He would be in touch with me later that morning. I decided to use the time to look around Umtata.

The Transkei capital looked thriving and prosperous. Every kind of business enterprise was represented, including automobile and farm machinery showrooms, supermarkets, banks, filling stations, and several hotels. All of them White-owned. No signs that Blacks had any kind of eco-

nomic foothold in this, their own community. I passed the
neat new police station, the white policeman leaning lazily
against the door, looking toward the new multistoried
Government buildings. Truly a thriving town, showing off
its potential for growth and development. Blacks everywhere, but not in command, not in authority. About half a
mile from the hotel I saw a charming single-storied building, evidently a school, attractive in its simplicity of design,
the large windows promising excellent natural lighting for
the rooms. A well-kept grassy playground occupied the
adjoining lot. On inquiring about it from a passerby I
learned that it was the white school—a school for the
children of white administrators and businessmen. Here in
the heart of a black enclave, the White-only restrictions still
applied. The charming bungalows, offices, shops, everything carried the invisible but unmistakable label, "White."

After lunch I set out, with the Information Officer, for
a tour of some parts of the Transkei. It could not be
accidental that this so-called black Homeland was, for the
most part, rocky, infertile land which can barely support
the local herdsmen's scrawny cattle and goats. Adjacent to
the township were many neat, small bungalows, silent
evidence of the social changes which have overtaken the
region, as the men are lured away from the small farm
holdings to the unskilled jobs in the township. The horse is
less in evidence than the car. Beyond the township the
bungalows gradually gave way to the traditional circular
Zulu huts of thatch and clay, each with its small patch of
maize; women working among the long rows of green
stalks, men tending their cows on sparsely covered hill-
sides. Even here, in their supposed "Homeland," Blacks
were literally restricted to the outer limits of the township,
out of sight of progress, needed only to grease its wheels.

The more I saw of the Transkei the more I sympathized with those urban blacks who were so determined to avoid being relocated to the Homelands. The Government's stated policy foresaw eventual independence for regions such as the Transkei. On what kind of economic base could such independence be founded? The businesses in Umtata were all White-owned, their profits surely siphoned out of the black community. I asked the Information Officer about this. He told me that the overall plan envisaged a gradual takeover of all businesses by Blacks. White businessmen were encouraged to employ Blacks and train them into the techniques of management. When a trainee showed himself capable of taking over, the Government could purchase the business from the owner at current market prices and resell it to the trainee-manager on extended terms. I remarked that I saw no sign of any Blacks being trained. The scheme was new, but was slowly getting under way, he claimed. I said that the places I'd visited all showed clear evidence of prosperity, and it seemed unlikely their owners would easily relinquish them. Umtata is the largest and busiest of the Transkei towns. I could not see the businessmen walking away from such a gold mine. He had no answer.

Everywhere we drove the situation was the same. Blacks following their "traditional lifestyle" on land which grudgingly and barely supported them. The more I saw the more absurd became the Government's claim that it was nurturing these Homelands toward independence. I reflected on the recent turbulent history of my own homeland, Guyana, and the years of preparation in the management of government and services. How could powerless people learn to exercise power wisely except through experience?

Back in Umtata, I took a stroll to a place which seemed to fulfill the joint purposes of bus stop, taxi stand, and open-air market. Only Blacks in sight. Overlooking this crossroads was an imposing new hotel. A fruit vendor told me that it was a new hotel for Blacks only, as they were not welcome at the other hotels. I didn't tell him where I was staying but, in reply to his question, admitted merely that I was an overseas visitor passing through the town. Inquisitively, two or three others strolled over to listen in on our conversation. I asked about the fruit on sale, tiny bananas, some hard peaches, and mangoes, and learned that they were grown on the patches of land tended by the vendors themselves. It was too early in the season for anything except bananas and peaches. They were surprised to discover that I knew about mangoes and could tell them about varieties familiar in the West Indies but which they'd never heard of.

Gradually, carefully, I steered the talk to independence, saying I'd heard in Johannesburg that the Transkei would become independent, and adding that perhaps some of them might be in the Government. This amused them.

"Who's been telling you those stories? Buthelezi?" one asked.

"I read it in the newspapers," I replied.

"The newspapers are not for African people. They say what the white man wants to hear."

"I read that this homeland will become independent as a separate state, like Botswana or Lesotho."

"I'll tell that to my grandchildren," one young man said, "and even then they will not believe it." He was about twenty years old. I suddenly realized that we were conversing easily in English. These rural Blacks were not educated men but they were able to converse with me in my language, and, most likely, they were as comfortable with Afrikaans. Now and then, they would revert to their tribal languages as if to underscore their linguistic range.

"What about you?" I asked. "Any of you preparing to be leaders?" saying it with a smile, making my inquiry sound casual and unimportant. Immediately there was that exchange of glances I'd come to recognize, and with it the withdrawal. Two of the young men walked away.

"Did you say you are from overseas?" the vendor asked.

"Yes. Why?"

"Sometimes strangers come here asking questions." Then turned to one of his companions and spoke in an African language which ignored and dismissed me. Even so tentative an inquiry about political activity had been enough to excite suspicion and distrust. People thinking of independence would be preparing for it, somehow, and there must be some evidence of that preparation. Perhaps, as the man said, it was all white newspaper talk.

Beyond the Transkei borders and into Natal, the countryside changed dramatically. The land was predominantly flat or rolling, perfect for farming on a vast scale. The road wound itself through lovely rural areas with attractive townships spaced between the wide expanses of farmland, mile upon mile of the lush green of wheat or maize, with here and there orchards heavy with oranges, peaches, or mangoes. The glow of prosperity lay over the neat, freshly painted bungalows with smooth, trimmed hedges and lawns. The modernistic spires of the calvinist kirks were a particularly dominant feature of each township. Wealth, comfort, and prosperity everywhere, the well-fed burghers chatting outside their houses, the ubiquitous black servants carefully sweeping, clipping, and tending.

Blacks everywhere in each town, manning the filling stations and delivery trucks, always in the servant roles, the local burghers slow-moving in their untroubled security, seeming hardly to see the Blacks who fetched and carried for them.

Outside Pietermaritzburg we needed directions for the shorter route to Durban and sought them at a police station. Two entrances to the same office, one for Blacks (all Non-Whites) and one for Whites. Three policemen standing outside, two 'Indians and one White. I approached the white one and asked directions to Durban. He merely stared past me, his pale eyes seeking some distant point beyond my shoulder. After a few moments I left him and returned to the car. My driver sought and received the information from the Indian policemen, the white one looking on. Perhaps the bastard thought himself too important even to speak to a black man. I wondered what kind of relationships obtained in that police station. We drove away.

My driver complained that I should not have spoken to the policeman, and said that, in his view, it would help me if I observed the "Black" and "White" signs where they appeared. He claimed that he did not support the Government's racial policies, arguing that he was of British stock. Yet he was obviously irritated with me for not falling in line. He predicted that, with my attitude, I'd have a rough time in Cape Town. I told him I'd be happy if he did the driving and left my behavior to me.

Returning to Durban, I telephoned several people, friends of Johannesburg friends, hoping to arrange meetings. They were all Indian, which was not surprising as most of the Indians in the country are located in Natal Province of which Durban is the capital. Indians were originally brought to South Africa as indentured laborers for the sugar plantations in much the same way as they were first taken to Guyana. In both countries they had prospered, emerging mainly as truck farmers, sugar cane planters, and small businessmen. Under the Nationalist Government their fortunes had altered dramatically and, though they still enjoyed a few privileges denied the black African, they were subject to many restrictions. Like other Non-Whites, they are consigned to enclaves and though unlike black Africans they are allowed to purchase land on which to build homes, they may at short notice be moved to some other location if the authorities decide that the one they occupy is more suitable or desirable for Whites. One of these Indian friends, a doctor, accepted my invitation to come and share some tea within the hour.

Punctually on the hour, my telephone rang. The doctor was calling from the lobby. She had arrived, but on entering the lobby, had been stopped and told that Non-Whites were not allowed in the hotel. She explained that she was calling on me and was eventually allowed to telephone my room. Angered, I went down to the lobby and without a word to anyone, escorted her up to my room. She seemed quite unperturbed by the experience, and wryly amused at my anger.

"I quite expected that they'd stop me," she said.

"Even when you said you were here to see me?"

"Sure. They have to remind us that the presence of a black visitor in the hotel really makes no difference. We are still not welcome. Anyway, welcome to Durban."

"Thank you. Shall we go down and have some tea?"

"I think it would be better if you had it sent up. I've had enough of white contempt for one day. Besides, we can talk more freely up here."

While waiting for our tea she told me of her practice among her people, many of whom were able to make a good living, in spite of the increasing restrictions placed upon them. She, like so many of her friends and clients, had been

born and raised in Durban where a thriving Indian community had developed. They had built a mosque and several
good schools, cinemas, a community center. About seven
years ago, the Government had rezoned that part of Durban where they lived and redesignated it a white area.
Except for some businesses, the Indians were to be relocated some miles out of Durban. Their homes would have to
be sold, either privately to Whites, or through compulsory
purchase by the Government. In either event, the purchase
price was frozen at the price obtaining when the order was
first announced. The Indians protested the order but they
had no political power base from which to make their
protest effective. She said that as a result of the order, many
families had become dislocated, and the community demoralized.

"If you'd like to come with me, I'll show you," she
offered. The tea arrived, we drank it and set off. We drove
about the Indian section of Durban while she pointed out a
house here, a bungalow or office there, all evacuated and
desolate awaiting either new white occupancy or the bull-
dozer which would level the lot for a new park or shopping
center. We visited an arcade where I was introduced to
some Indian traders, nearly inarticulate in their bewilder-
ment and frustration.

"Is there no way of protesting these orders?" I asked.

"It is dangerous for Blacks to protest," I was told. "All
it could bring you would be a cell in jail, or, at best, a
cracked head."

I was struck by this Indian doctor's inclusive use of the
word "Blacks," especially in a country where shades of
color were so important in determining where one lived, or
worked. Perhaps it was her way of responding to my
sympathetic interest.

"Have you heard?" someone interposed, excitedly. "They're rioting out at New Germany."

"Who's rioting?" I inquired.

"The Blacks at Frames."

"What's Frames?" I asked the doctor.

"It's a textile factory complex, with plants scattered around Durban. Cheap black labor, Indian and African, at starvation wages. Seems the workers have gone on strike. Something must have happened out there to make the workers risk a confrontation with the police and their guns and their dogs."

"Where's this New Germany?"

"In the suburbs. Not far away. Would you like to go out there?"

"Could we?"

"Oh, we could. The important thing would be to keep well away from any trouble areas, but it would be an eye-opener for you if your stomach can take it. The police can be quite brutal, you know."

I assured her that my stomach would be fine and we drove off toward New Germany and the Seltex factory. My friend told me that nearly ten thousand workers were employed at ten factories around Durban, five of them owned by the Frames company, reportedly notorious for their bad working conditions.

Even before I caught sight of the factory, we could hear the sound of human voices, a loud, unintelligible rumble punctuated by shouts. Around a bend in the road, we saw a large number of Blacks milling about in front of the main office building, and my friend pulled the car onto the grass verge, well away from the action. We got out and walked to a point of vantage some distance away from the crowds but with a clear view of what was taking place.

Several police vans were parked in an orderly row, and near them stood several groups of policemen, both black and white, some holding large dogs on the leash, others carrying walkie-talkies or armed with riot helmets, nightsticks, and rifles or Sten guns. A few dogs were straining at their leashes, but most of them sat obediently at the heels of their handlers.

We moved to the outer edge of the crowd to find out what had happened. My friend beckoned two Indian workers who came over to speak with us. They said that the situation was very explosive. The strike had been in progress since early morning and, so far, nearly four hundred workers had been arrested and carried off. Similar strikes were in progress at factories in Pinetown and Hammarsdale, all located within the environs of Durban.

From some of the workers I was able to get the story of the circumstances which led to the strike. They had long been promised a pay raise, ranging from ten cents to two Rand per week, depending on length of service. When they received their latest pay envelopes it was discovered that management had reneged on the promise. Such conduct by management was familiar, but the decision to strike was spontaneous and unexpected.

The law of South Africa expressly forbids strikes by Blacks, and only very grudgingly nowadays allows them limited negotiating action. In striking the men were risking prosecution, especially under the vague but comprehensively punitive Suppression of Communism Act. I noticed, here and there among the crowd, white men in civilian clothes equipped with cameras and recording devices. I was told that they were members of the Security Police, collecting information for use in later prosecution of individuals.

The workers had reported for work as usual at 6:00 A.M. but had refused to go into the factory. Management had promptly called the police who arrived in their vans within minutes and stationed themselves in full, threatening view of the workers, waiting for any provocation. I noticed two Whites, a man and a woman, both civilians, moving among the Blacks, talking and quietly exhorting small groups. I was told that they were labor union organizers, advising the Blacks to continue to strike until better pay and working conditions were negotiated. In so doing, they were breaking the law, on several counts, and my informants assured me that, eventually, they would be severely punished.

Why eventually, I wanted to know.

"Probably any attempt to arrest them here would ignite the already volatile situation, beyond any power of control by the police. However, the police will get those two—later."

Suddenly the police were moving forward, in a spaced line, the dog handlers in the vanguard. The black officers seemed as ruthless and brutal as their white comrades. The crowd fell back before them. From the front ranks of the crowd a young black man broke away, hat in hand, moving toward the edge of the crowd. In an instant a police dog was loosed, swiftly and silently overtaking him. As the crowd roared in protest, he looked backward, stumbled and fell. The dog seized him by the bare forearm, worrying it from side to side as the young man screamed. The dog's handler reached the young man, roughly dragged him upright before snapping the leash onto the snarling animal, which reluctantly let go of his arm.

The young man had in no way threatened anyone. He was now roughly handled toward one of the police vans and shoved inside. The crowd kept up its noisy protests as the police continued their steady advance. Suddenly, without a sound, one of them clutched his face in both hands

and fell forward. Someone whispered that he had been
struck by a stone. The advancing police stopped and two of
them rushed to help their brother officer. To my amaze-
ment, several black workers left the crowd and knelt to help
the stricken policeman, gently cradling his head on their
knees. Two policemen quickly brought a stretcher and
placed their comrade on it, brushing aside the helpful
Blacks.

The injured policeman safely away in an ambulance,
the police continued their advance on the crowd until it was
encircled on three sides.

"Start thinking up a story to explain why you're here,"
the doctor whispered to me. "Just in case they come this
way." A young black worker came over to us.

"You reporters?" he asked.

"No. Just strangers, looking on," I said.

"Strangers from where? Durban?"

"No, from overseas. I heard about the strike and came
along to see what was happening."

"This isn't a strike," he said. "It's a set up. The big
boss Frame has been promising a raise for weeks, then they
said we'd have it last Friday. So we get our pay and it's the
same as always. No raise. So we walk out and they bring in
the police. Always the same. They're saying that the news
from the other factories is the same. I just heard that the
Minister for Community Affairs of the Kwa-Zulu Homeland is on his way here for a meeting with management
representatives."

"Is he white?"

"No, he's black."

"Don't you have any local representatives to negotiate
with management?" I asked him.

"Representatives? The police look to see who's doing

the talking and they pick him up. Sometimes the police send in their spies among us to start us talking, then they come along and pick us up. What about you? Suppose they find you here?" he asked me.

"Suppose who finds me here?"

"The Security Police."

"Well, I'm not interfering. Just looking on. The most they can do is ask me to leave."

"Don't be too sure. You're black. They could rough you up first and ask who you are later. In any case, my friend, when you move, walk. Never run. They're always looking out for black men running." With that cryptic remark, he wandered off.

It was frightening. All of it. The bewildered Blacks temporarily courageous in the rightness of their cause; invisible management exploiting their weakness; and the big brutal police, ready, willing, and able to wield their power. Helen Suzman's daughter was right—it seemed as if the Blacks were being deliberately harried toward breaking point. The time must soon come, I told myself, when no show of police strength would be enough to contain the workers' explosive anger and destructive rage.

Early next morning, I left by plane for Cape Town, after promising to route myself once more through Durban on my return journey to Johannesburg. Arrived at Cape Town I booked into the President Hotel at Sea Point. I had hardly settled into my room when the Assistant Manager came to see me, apologizing for what he had to tell me. It appeared that when my reservation had been requested by telephone from Johannesburg, he, knowing who I was, had applied for and received a permit allowing the reservation. However, the permit was granted on condition that I, a black man, did not use the bar at the same time as white patrons. He said he way sorry to inform me of that proscription, but he had no choice in the matter.

I was furious and told him so. I was paying for my accommodation at the same rate as anyone else and warned him that if I wanted to take a drink in the bar at any time, I would do so. Either he accepted my reservation or he did not, but if he did I demanded to be treated exactly the same as any other guest. He showed me a copy of the letter and permit issued by the Interior Ministry. I asked for copies of both so that I could study them and he promised to let me have them, but never did.

Next day, Mr. Englebrecht MP, whom I'd met a year ago in New York, called for me and, with his wife, took me on a leisurely tour along the shoreline of Cape Town. As we talked I tried to measure his political acumen and sophistication. An Afrikaner, he had been a schoolmaster before entering politics as a supporter of the Nationalist Party and seemed to be in complete agreement with the Government's racial policies. To my critical remarks on the education, housing, and employment of Blacks he replied that the Bantu Act and similar laws were designed specifically for the benefit of Blacks. It became clear that, to him, Blacks are intellectually and psychologically inferior to Whites.

He spoke of how Blacks lived in the rural Homelands, the women in servitude, tending the fields while rearing children, the men content in continual idleness except for the little effort required to tend their cattle, sheep or goats. I asked how, if that were the general rule, the mines and other industries were able to recruit all the black workers they needed. Were the Blacks impressed into service like the sailors of old?

He complained that outsiders were far too eager to

criticize South Africa without fully appreciating the prevailing situation. Few of the critics had even visited the
country as I was doing for a firsthand view. The Blacks, he
believed, were, for the most part, content with their circumstances, and would be quite responsive to gradual
improvements, were they let alone and not incited to strikes
and other anti-social actions by activists, often from outside.
(An outsider from where? The only outsiders with easy
access to South Africa are the British. Perhaps that's what
he meant.) The Government was aware of such activities
and had the means to stop them.

Evolution, not revolution, he reminded me, and
referred pityingly to the parlous state of the British economy which was crippled perhaps beyond repair by strikes
which were all, he believed, Communist inspired. That
would never happen in South Africa. In any case, he
believed that many people in Britain were disillusioned
with conditions there and were thinking of emigrating to
South Africa. I argued that though many young people
were leaving Britain, South Africa was lowest among their
choices of a new home, and suggested that the near inevita-
bility of bloody confrontation between Black and White
might be responsible. He said that such a confrontation was
most unlikely, because it would not be allowed to happen.
His haughty assurance was disturbing. How could anyone
with any claim to sensitivity be so determined to ignore all
the ominous signs? Or was he only saying those things to
me? In the time I'd already spent in the country, I'd already
heard and seen enough to convince me that events were
moving, however slowly, to some awful, cataclysmic
dénouement. Perhaps this man and his wife, so comfortable
under the prevailing system, were really reassuring themselves that it would continue. At least for their lifetime. I
then remembered that, when I had first met Englebrecht at

a cocktail party in New York, he had told me that he was one of the group of censors in South Africa who had voted to ban the showing of the film of my autobiography, *To Sir, with Love*. When I'd asked him the reason for the ban, he'd replied,

"As we watched that film at a private showing, we were all irritated by the sight of that black teacher being so right all the time."

"What do you mean by being right?" I'd asked.

"Well, being so knowledgeable, so bright, setting the example for white students."

"But the film was eventually released to the public."

"Yes, with a change here and there."

I wondered if he was remembering that I was that same teacher in person, unchanged, still willing to make my small challenge to social absurdities.

We stopped for tea at a teashop and sat at one of the outdoor tables. When the black waiter served our tea he asked me if I was the same person whose photograph was in the morning newspaper. I said I was. He told me he'd read *To Sir* and would like me to autograph his personal copy of the paperback edition. I wondered if my companions appreciated the implication. As long as people could think and read, there was no knowing what they might do, for themselves. Perhaps the small miracle needed to change the course of events in South Africa was already on its way.

8

Later that week I met with the Deputy Minister for Bantu Education. Formerly a dominie in the Reformed Dutch Church, he spoke of Blacks as if they were a lesser breed of man whose collective course must be carefully plotted and controlled by those whom God had elected their masters, the Whites. Painstakingly he detailed the many and varied educational programs he claimed were designed to help Blacks function in the South African society, and made it seem that huge sums of money were spent annually to that purpose. Courteously he brushed aside my suggestion that if the proscriptions against multi- and interracial education were removed, education for all might be less costly.

"Our Blacks are incapable of learning at the same pace as Whites," he told me, smiling his pontifical smile as if he knew he was quoting Holy Writ. "They need to be helped, slowly and carefully."

"Toward what level?" I asked.

"Toward their own level. It would be foolish to place them in any educational situation beyond their limited potential."

"I've discovered that under previous governments,

Blacks attended your universities and gave an excellent account of themselves. In those days their potential was never in question."

"You were misinformed," he disagreed, still smiling. "In those days there were those who experimented with the educational process and were anxious to prove themselves right. Many of our Blacks were frustrated by a university experience specifically designed for Whites. This Government has learned from those mistakes."

"I'm thinking of my own university education," I told him. "At no time did I feel frustrated by it or incompetent to deal with it."

"You cannot compare your background with that of our Bantu." Nothing seemed likely to disturb his composure. "I've dealt with them all my life. As you move about through our country and see them, I'm sure you will appreciate the difference between them and yourself." He stood up in dismissal.

Next was a luncheon with Mr. Englebrecht and some of his fellow MPs, who were gathered and waiting for me in a small, private dining room in the House. When the introductions were made, I realized that they were all of the ruling Nationalist Party, and as we settled into conversation, I noticed how eager each seemed to prove his party loyalty and political savvy. One of them had recently "crossed over" from the opposition United Party.

"Would that be a case of political defection?" I needled him.

"Not at all. For as long as I shared the views and objectives of the United Party members, I worked in pursuit of those objectives. But political attitudes should be responsive to the people's interests, and the United Party is philosophically behind the times. I believe in this country and its destiny so I joined the party whose objectives and vision matched mine."

He was going to some lengths to convince me that his move was not dictated by political opportunism. I wondered about his constituents. English parliamentarians seemed generally flexible in the face of political realities. These South Africans, without exception, demonstrated an unfailing inflexibility, making me wonder if it was because they dared not drift from the rigid philosophical center, for fear of being labeled liberal, the political kiss of death. They spoke of their country and its people, but left me in no doubt that they meant white people and were completely insensitive to the plight of anyone else. They seemed to believe that their political supremacy would last forever and that no effort by the Blacks inside or anyone else outside could reverse the situation.

There were no political signs to contradict them. Their main opposition, the United Party, was torn by internal strife and, in fact, offered no realistic alternative platforms. Differing only in degree, the United Party's attitude to Blacks was paternalistic and repressive, as they were careful to avoid any progressive recommendations beyond the minimal sops to overseas criticisms. The brand new Nationalist was in his element, an enthusiastic convert among those diehards. He suggested that South Africa's policies were hardly different from those practiced in some parts of the United States.

I countered this by saying that I was currently on the faculty of a Southern university and had discovered that some of the most adventurously progressive changes in American social and educational attitudes were taking place in the South. Whereas a few years ago Southern American Blacks were denied even the right to vote, today they were competing for and sometimes being elected to high office, including that of mayor and could soon be expected to aim higher, much higher.

Lest there be any misunderstanding of where I stood, I

reminded them that I was a native of a country of Blacks, governed by Blacks, descendants of slaves and indentured laborers. As I walked and drove around their country, I could discover no genetic difference between the black South Africans and myself, and felt confirmed in my confidence that I was the equal of anyone, black or white.

They remained courteously adamant, refusing even to consider the existence of any parallels. They believed they were in the right, the God-given right of Afrikaners who understood their place in Africa and were not interested in references to other, distant situations. They made no attempt to support their positions by argument. Each one would make a statement, either well-rehearsed or familiar through frequent use, and the others would express complete agreement. The wonder of it all was that they were saying it to me.

I examined my own reactions to them. They were bigots, just like others I had met in other countries. Their bigotry was no less offensive to me because they were South African. On the contrary. How could they imagine that I, in my black skin, was different from the Blacks all around them? If they knew that the native Blacks feared and hated them and would seize the opportunity to be revenged on them, why did they assume that I would feel differently?

Maybe they really didn't give a damn about what I thought or how I felt. Maybe their sitting, eating, and talking with me was the real measure of their contempt. I was black. In these near-intimate circumstances they could tell me and show me what they felt about the millions of Blacks like me whom they ruled with cruelty and contempt, enforced by banning, restriction, imprisonment, and death.

I asked them about their political opposition in general and Mrs. Helen Suzman in particular. Their responses demonstrated their complete confidence in the power of their party and in the prevailing national indifference. They showed little respect for Mrs. Suzman's politics but were eager to claim her as proof of the Government's ability to accommodate criticism. Could these men ever conceive of relinquishing this enormous power or sharing it with Blacks?

On returning to my hotel, I received a telephone call from someone who introduced himself as Mr. Welcome Msomi. He told me that he knew of me, had heard and read of my presence in South Africa, was an ardent fan especially after reading *Reluctant Neighbors* with which he fully identified, and wished to invite me to a performance of the Zulu Theatre Company's version of *Macbeth*, or, in Zulu, *Umabatha*, written in Zulu by Mr. Msomi himself, who also played the lead. I promptly accepted the invitation.

Umabatha was staged at the Maynardville Open Air Theatre. The aged, gnarled trees which ringed the grassy stage were an ideal background for the grim events of Shakespeare's bloody tragedy. From the opening moments when the three witches emerged leaping and shrieking from the cavernous dark between the trees, through the spectacular tribal dances, the plotting to kill Duncan (Dungane) and Banquo (Bhangane) and their deaths, and the final defeat and death of Macbeth (Babatha), the audience was held enthralled.

Such was the vigor of the play that, though I understood not a single word of Zulu, I was irresistibly carried along with its flow, its pace, its power, and above all the natural way in which it blended into its element, the starlit, African night. Whether crossing the stage in military elegance, spears closely aligned to present a colorful phalanx, bare feet pounding rhythms from the green turf, or leaping at each other in angry confrontation, the actors filled the stage with movement, now vibrant, now attenuated as death itself. Towering above all was Umabatha, power-hungry yet fearful, a willing pawn in the hands of his ambitious, resourceful wife, magnificently played by Daisy Dumakudi, who drew repeated cheers from the audience.

At the end of the performance, I made a surprising discovery. Beside me was a black couple, and we introduced ourselves and chatted for a few moments before the curtain went up. On the other side of me and in front were Whites, and I had felt pleased that there was no discrimination in this theatre. But looking around at the end, when the lights came up, I saw that behind me for a few rows were a group of seats occupied by Blacks, so, together we were a tiny enclave in the white audience, altogether little more than a score of black faces, but grouped together. Was it purely accidental that the only seat available was in exactly that spot? I'll never know, but it is possible to stretch the long arm of coincidence too far. I told myself to think only of the joy of the evening.

After the show, I was introduced to the organizers, Mrs. Renée Ahrenson and Mrs. Cecelia Sonnenberg, and the black cast. In the men's dressing room they gathered about me, enveloping me with their enthusiastic welcome, telling me I was Zulu, my face, build, everything. They'd read and talked about my books, especially *Reluctant Neighbors*, because they knew from immediate and painful experience about white contempt for the black man. They appreciated the irony of this very evening, cheered so enthusiastically tonight by Whites who would not look at them in the street tomorrow.

"We are like court jesters," one said, "entertaining them at their command, compensated by the scraps from their table."

Even among the gaiety of our meeting the pervasive

bitterness was there, yet it could not dampen their spirit or inhibit their determination to pursue their profession. They talked of other plays by Shakespeare and other playwrights which they planned to examine for their translatability into the fluid, powerful Zulu. One young actor asked me about my stay in Cape Town, about my movements, and whether I was being followed. He hinted that he would like to come to my hotel to talk with me privately. I told him I had no way of knowing if I was followed, but, if he was willing to take the risk, I'd be pleased to talk with him at my hotel.

"Ride back with me to the hotel," I invited.

"No," he replied. "I must go back to town with the others, but I could come to see you tomorrow morning."

"Come and have breakfast with me."

"Okay. Around nine?"

"Fine."

He arrived a little before nine next morning, with three others from the *Umabatha* cast. We ordered breakfast and I told them how deeply impressed I had been by their performance the night before. Tremendous.

"Sure. For the Whites," one said.

"*I* enjoyed it," I reminded them.

"Yes. We understand that. But who do you think benefits from it? The black actors and actresses? Never. Did you hear what happened to them in London? Same rave reviews. Same sold-out performances. Yet there wasn't enough money to pay the boys' hotel bills. Did you know that? Welcome might be doing all right, but what about the others? If it had been a white company with white actors on such a successful run, everybody would have been doing fine, *Umabatha's* a black company, of black actors. But the management is white. The Whites are doing nicely with the production. Only the Blacks are having a rough time."

I needed to know where all this was leading, so I said nothing.

"We hear you've talked with some of the boys, some poets you met here in town, and that you might be writing about it. So we'd like you to get the story straight."

"What story?"

"The story about how helpless the black man is in this country. You'll hear about the black poet and the black musician and the black writer and the black actor. We're all slaves, my friend. You know how ants keep aphids to milk them. It's that way with the black artist. If he has any talent he's milked by some white bastard until he's dry. That's how this country is. A black man cannot talk with publishers or promoters or people like that, so he has to have a white man to do it for him. So the white man takes over. He doesn't really represent the black artist, doesn't work for him. He becomes the boss. He calls the tune. He is the employer instead of the servant. He pays what suits him. The Black sweats his ass out. He creates. He writes. He directs. But at the end of it all, he's never mentioned in the program notes. Whitey takes Blackey to London, Tokyo, Perth. He fills his bank account with loot and the black man returns home with nothing."

"Wait a minute," I said, and picked up the *Umabatha* program. "Look here. Welcome's mentioned quite prominently as originator, writer, and leading man."

"Shit, man. Have you talked with him? Sure his name is in the book, but who do you think reaps the harvest? Welcome thinks he's doing okay, but what about all the others in the cast? He couldn't do it alone."

I wondered about that, trying to relate what these men were saying to the exuberance and enthusiasm I'd just witnessed. Was it possible for unhappy, dissatisfied players to perform with such verve? What was that line so familiar in the theater? The play's the thing. Perhaps it was true here in Africa, here among Blacks who considered themselves as professional as any Shakespearean specialist.

"Like all men, the black artist has to eat, my friend," one said. "He has to have a family, he needs a decent roof, needs to buy material for his craft and all that. The white man knows all this, selects his talented lamb and draws him to the slaughterhouse. The throat is cut and the blood is drawn until the carcass is useless."

"Wait a moment," I interrupted. "How do you know all this?"

They exchanged glances with each other, and a few words in their own language. Then one said:

"We're artists. We're still students as every artist is always a student. We do different things, but we're all caught in the white man's snare. Without him we're helpless, we don't eat. With him we're meat which he slices as he wishes. The system protects him as he ravages our flesh. He smells out our talents before we're aware of it, then he sells our talent for his benefit. He becomes the agent. In the case of a painter or sculptor, he offers the work to galleries in the cities where we couldn't get into the door without his help, then he prices the work and takes the biggest slice. In the case of a musician, there is the recording studio. The white agent negotiates and often winds up owning the copyright. Sometimes his name appears on the record as composer. Same thing with live performances. I've yet to hear of a black musician earning thirty Rand a performance in spite of a full house."

The faces around me were now grim, bitter masks, the suppressed hatred of years spilling out with their words.

"You write books, my friend, and you get the credit. They make movies of your work and you get the credit and the money. You can come here and live in a hotel like this, a big room like this. In your country you can be a real artist. Here we are shit."

A waiter wheeled our breakfast into the room, looking with some surprise at me and my guests. I told him we'd help ourselves, tipped him, and he left.

"You have an agent?" one asked. "What's he like? Black? White?"

"White and she's a woman."

"I hear that over there you pay the agent a percentage. Right?"

"Right."

"Here the man who represents you pays you something—or nothing. What we tell ourselves all the time is 'Come together. Close ranks. End the squabbles among ourselves. Stop underselling each other. Let's find our direction, present what *we* want, where *we* want it and *how* we want it.' How will we achieve this? By striving for good standards like the white man did. By working at perfecting our art, not for any exotic superficialities, but for quality. Shit, the white man was not born with his high standards. He worked for them. We can work for them too. Not his, but our own."

I liked what they were saying and felt my reservations evaporating rapidly.

"How will you achieve all this?" I asked.

"By working together, supporting each other. By accepting hunger and pain until we can speak for ourselves, negotiate for ourselves. Some of our brothers have formed an organization. Mdali, in Johannesburg. Its purpose is to get all our people involved in discovering our talents and our arts. Up to now we've been preoccupied with showing off our talents and our arts to the white man, selling ourselves to him. Now we must forget that shit. We must take our art and talent to our people in the ghettos. If and when our art is good enough, the white man will come to us. In the ghettos. He will watch us perform among our people and will respect our people because he'll have to respect all of it. The art and the people."

"Listen, friend," one said. "When we talk of supporting our own, we are talking more to ourselves than to you. The habits of eating, of warm clothing, of sleeping under a roof with a woman make slaves of us all. I am also a sculptor and after years of work, what do I have to show? Nothing. No house, no money, no clothes, no wife, no studio, no kiln!" The last words said in a sudden shout as he jumped up from his seat and walked over to stare outside through the sunlit window. The others looked over at him but made no move to go to him.

"Friend," one said. "We came to talk with you as a fellow artist, not to burden you with our pain. We really came to talk to you about acting and writing prose and poetry, and painting pictures and carving wood. But here we are sharing our pain with you. We look at you, at how you live here, the confidence with which you speak and we envy you. You are an artist, independent. That's why this government lets you come into this country, into this hotel. We want to be independent as artists. Independent of the white man, employing him only as we need him. We envy you. Look at me. Until coming into this room I've told myself I needed the white man, because he stood between me and the door. Every door. Now I feel I can promise the white man that I don't really need him, have never needed him. I should have known it all the time."

"Brother," another said. "You see, we're now talking for ourselves. Each one for his work. We're actors because we need to eat. Each of us is something else. Something individual. Ben's a sculptor and gets very little for the work he does, then later sees pictures of his pieces in glossy magazines. Not even his name to them. Same thing with Biki's painting. Tom and me, we write. Some poetry, some prose. I would have liked to go on to the university to study literature, but that's a dream. Me, when the frustration gets me, I drown myself in brandy. If I can afford it. Like my brothers here, I want a chance to exhibit, to expose myself to the world, to compete. But what can I do here. *Vokol.* Nothing."

"Anything I can do?" I asked.

"You're doing it, brother," one said. "You invited us to come and talk with you. You listen. We heard about you but we needed to see and hear you for ourselves. We've seen Blacks from your country come here before. Bob Foster for one. He stayed here, hidden from us behind his managers and secretaries. We weren't sure about you. Come see us in Jo'burg. Come to Mdali and meet some more of the brothers. Will you?"

I promised I would. I remembered my early suspicion and distrust. Now I felt humbled. I could think of nothing to say to reach and touch them, to convey my oneness with them and their plight, for anything I said would merely emphasize my own fortunate position.

I thought of suggesting that they flee the country and try their fortune in some more sympathetic society, but swallowed the words before they could leak out. These men were talking of developing themselves, proving themselves among their own people in their own land.

I poured coffee and drank to them. To the cast of *Umabatha*, to those isolated on Robben Island, to Mdali, to Blacks everywhere involved in the struggle for freedom and dignity.

"And you with us, brother," they said.

9

On my return to Johannesburg, I accepted an invitation to address the members of the Executive of the Young Women's Christian Association in Soweto. Two members of the Executive, Mrs. Meteni and Mrs. Iowele, called for me at the hotel and visited for a few minutes. Both housewives, both married to men who worked in Johannesburg, they told me that their YWCA branch was all black, in keeping with the Government's segregationist policies. Both had attended YWCA conferences outside South Africa and sat in the same room with delegates from the white South African branch.

"Did that cause you any difficulty?" I asked.

"Not us. We are not the ones who hold ourselves separate. Outside this country we meet as equals."

"Do overseas organizations know that here in South Africa you are kept separate?"

"Of course they do, but they cannot interfere."

On the way to their meeting room they took me through a part of Soweto I had not previously seen to show me, they said, the reasons why the YWCA served a useful purpose in the community. Women everywhere, many of them with very young children.

"Each day, except Sundays, Soweto becomes a community of women. The men are away at work, so most of us are left to clean house, tend the children, and watch the days slip away with little or nothing accomplished. We don't get any satisfaction from recounting our common miseries. Whatever improvement is needed here must come from us. The Bantu Council meets and talks but nothing happens, because all money decisions must be made by Whites in Johannesburg. So we've begun. Out of money we raised ourselves, through dances and picnics and collections, we've built one meeting hall. It's a beginning."

When we reached the meeting hall, I understood what she meant. It was a squat, L-shaped, solidly built red-brick structure, set on a small rise, the interstices between the bricks highlighted in white. Larger than any of its neighbors, it exuded an aura of elegance and permanence. The grass around it was neatly trimmed, and here and there recently transplanted trees stood like symbols of growth and hope.

"What do you think?" Mrs. Iowele asked, proudly.

"Very impressive," I replied.

"It's been eleven years in getting to this stage," Mrs. Meteni said. "When we can, we hope to add wings on either side of the main hall. Might take another eleven years, but we'll do it."

We went in and I was introduced to the other members. We sat down and they quickly and professionally attended to their business, reviewing their work among the young people, housewives and pre-school children of Soweto. From time to time their comments clearly indicated their separateness from the Whites, especially when they referred to invitations received to attend overseas conferences. They spoke of several fund-raising projects planned for the months ahead.

Their agenda completed, they invited me to address them. At this moment, two other women joined us, one of them white. Someone sitting next to me explained that she was a graduate student from an American university who was examining the social conditions in Soweto as a basis for a doctoral thesis. I spoke briefly, of the reason for my visit to South Africa and what I had so far seen as I traveled about the country.

Afterward, they spoke about Soweto and about the very few options open to black women. A few were teachers, some were nurses, or helpers at the local nursery schools, and many were domestics. All were frustrated by the narrowness of their lives.

"We read the YWCA publications sent to us from overseas," one said. "We read of the things women do, are allowed to do, in other countries, in other parts of Africa and here we are, forced to confine our interests and ambitions to Soweto, and, even so, what we do here depends on what the white man lets us do."

Suddenly one of the group, a graying, buxom woman stood up, interrupting the others with, "Sisters, we are wasting time, our own and that of our visitor. Let's not talk about the stupid irritations like where we can or cannot go. He didn't come all the way from America to hear that. Let's tell him about what's really important to us. Let's tell him about the thing which frightens us and keeps us helpless. Let's tell him about our Fear."

She seemed to capitalize the word, giving it a dimension of immediate threat, bringing it into the room with us. Looking directly at me she said, "My brother, we women live in Fear, every moment of every day of our lives. So do our men, but they, most of them, go off to work each morning and can temporarily forget their Fear in doing their jobs. But we think of them at those jobs and we fear for them. I have a man, sir, a lovely man, a good man who looks after me and our children. He's a very intelligent man. I know, because I live with him. I love to hear him talk with me and the children or with our friends when they come to visit. I'm very proud of him." She paused and looked around at the others, all with their eyes focused on her.

"My man works as an ordinary clerk in the city, a job any boy could do, but he has no way of seeking or getting promotion. Young white boys order him about, calling him 'boy' sometimes. My man. My proud man. It's eating away at him inside."

One of the women who had come to my hotel looked questioningly at me, as if wondering whether I wanted to hear what her colleague was saying. I nodded affirmatively.

"I watch my man go off at five each morning, and I wonder whether today will be the day when the dam will break, when somebody will say the final word to him, when some Whitey will heap on his head the final indignity and my man will lose control." Some of the others were nodding their heads as she spoke, their faces grave, living with her in her pain.

"It will happen one day," she went on. "I can feel it in my bones, because I know my man. One day they will say something or do something to him and he will blow up. Do you know what will happen then to him, to us? They will call the police and take my man to jail, and I won't know anything about it. I will wait for him and when night comes and he is not here, I'll know. And the children will know. And tomorrow I must go search for him.

"Do you think the police will come to tell me my man is in jail? Never. I must search for him. One by one I must visit the police stations and ask for him. Always I must wait. I must swallow my anxiety and wait while they look at me, hating me because my husband is a man, laughing at me because I am black and helpless. I must wait until they check their lists. Sometimes they spell his name or pronounce his name their way and do not recognize the name I give them, so they say 'Go. We do not have your man.'"

The room was quiet yet vibrant with the spell of the woman's pain. It seemed as if it was there with us, happening before our eyes.

"So, day after day I must search, living with my Fear, living with my children who will draw upon my Fear and be frightened. Maybe in three or four days I'll find him, thrown into a stinking cell with many others, stinking with his shit and his Fear, as frightened as I am. The police will say 'Bring forty Rand to pay your husband's fine.' Forty Rand! It's as easy to tell me go steal a star from the sky. Without forty Rand my husband may be deported somewhere up North. Somehow I must get that money. So it is, my brother. We busy ourselves with this place, and whatever we can do here, to distract us from our Fear, for our men, for our children and for ourselves."

Her voice broke but her eyes were dry, though I knew she was weeping behind her eyes. The looks on the other faces told me they were with her on every frightening step she took.

"There's something else," she went on. "We also live in fear of each other. Look at us. All black. All poor. And yet, even among us, sisters you might say, there may be one or more who will later report to the Security Police about what has been said here, by you and by us, but especially by us. So, while we fear for each other, we go in fear of each other, selling each other for the puny privilege of a pass, a permit for a relative, or, worst of all, a few Rand. I read some of your books, my brother. You are a teacher. Tell us how to trust each other. That's what we need to know. Talk to us about trusting each other, because when we can trust each other, we can together be strong against the white man's tyranny."

I was about to reply, thinking that she was finished, but she lifted a hand to bid me wait.

"The white man wants to keep us afraid. Do you know how he does it? Ask anyone here. The Security Police raid our homes. Everyone's homes. It's to see if anyone's living there illegally, without a pass. They always come late at night or very early in the morning when we are dazed by sleep. They pound on our doors to frighten us, and if we're not quick to open them, they break them in. They love to see us huddled in our beds, cowering against their flash-lights and their guns. And their dogs. They love to pull the bedclothes off us and look at our nakedness. So we live, my brother. In spite of all that we've come together and built this place. Now tell us how we can build ourselves, that we might be stronger than our fear."

Abruptly she sat down, leaving me weakly unequal to the challenge of responding to her, to them.

"My sisters," I said, letting the moment and the feeling dictate whatever I'd say to them, "you've opened doors to a world I'd never known existed. I've lived in countries where Blacks must fight for everything they get and have, and in my own struggle I had imagined myself confronted with formidable difficulties. In the face of what I've heard today, I feel humble. I believe that people who suffer as you do and survive as you do, can discover in yourselves reasons to trust each other. It must have taken great courage for our sister to speak the way she did, and I would like to believe that we all respect that courage. Perhaps, at times, our personal, private needs seem greater than the collective good and I can only be sympathetic with those who must make choices under these terrible conditions. Be patient with each other."

Before leaving I talked informally with them, especially the matron who had spoken so eloquently and moved me so deeply. I loved her, the dignity and majesty limned in her smooth black face and I knew that the spirit of freedom glowed strongly in her and could ignite the feebler ones. I felt encouraged and strengthened.

Back at the hotel I was overcome by restlessness. I missed the casual ease of consorting with my friends in the U.S.A. and the challenge of my work. Here and now I was surrounded by hate and anger and menace and people engulfed in suffering. From my window I could see groups of young men scattered about the park and suddenly decided to go down among them.

I chose a group at random and sat on the grass nearby, within easy earshot, looking at them, evidently taking an interest. They were conversing in an African language, very animatedly, waving arms, sometimes jumping up the better to emphasize a point. I was fascinated by it all, and by the realization of being so much the outsider, not understanding a word of what went on.

Suddenly one of them noticed me and said something. I shook my head, smiling, and explained that I was a visitor from overseas, staying across the street at the Landdrost Hotel. They looked at me in surprise, then at the hotel and suddenly gathered around me, bombarding me with questions, in English. Suddenly one of them remembered reading something about me in one of the newspapers and asked if I was the author of *Reluctant Neighbors.* He had not read it but knew someone who had, and remembered some of the things discussed in it. For a while, we talked about me and my books, but gradually they got back to what they had been talking about before. It was the letter-bomb murder of Abraham Tiro in Gabarone, Botswana.

Mr. Tiro, self-exiled in Botswana, had formerly been the leader of one student organization, and was, at the time of his death, president of another. In a recent letter Mr. Tiro had affirmed their joint solidarity and had concluded with the enigmatic line, "No struggle can come to an end without casualties."

Hardly noticing me, they continued the discussion in English, arguing that the assassination was engineered by agents of the South African Security Forces, because Mr. Tiro had cleverly eluded them and fled to Botswana. The letter-bomb, according to them, was a highly sophisticated Western device, far removed from the kind of thing any African would ever think of using against another African. Furthermore, it was another attempt by the South African Security Forces to intimidate Africans by showing how capable they were of reaching their quarry, no matter where they hid. Suddenly, one of them pounded his fists on the ground, his face distorted with an anger he could barely contain.

"Look at us," he cried, "just look at us. Do you know what we're doing? We're mourning a brother. The white man has murdered our brother in Botswana and we are mourning him. But even that we must do here, in the open, away from prying eyes and ears. Why do we live like this? Our brother is dead. He killed no one, harmed no one. He merely spoke of the imperative of human dignity. He only spoke out against white brutality, and for that he was hunted and hounded from his school, his home, his country, and now his life. They watch us, his mourners, listening for some sign of protest. They let us know they're watching us, to make us fearful. And yet they say they fear us. They say we outnumber them and they fear us. From outside you are likely to believe them. Think of it. Twenty million Blacks against about four million Whites. From outside you will think of those numbers and their imbalance and you will believe that the white man really lives in fear of us. From outside you cannot see the way in which we are dispersed and weakened. Effective resistance is not established overnight. It needs to be planned, nurtured, and led. We need to see leaders, to give to any movement a point of reference. We need to know a man, with a name that we can talk about to our wives, our children, ourselves. We need to see our pride, clearly, in the flesh, to be reminded who we were and could be.

"We are ashamed, my friend, to sit here like women and weep for those whom they ban and imprison and kill. We, the sons of sons of Zulu warriors sit and cry because we are powerless in our fear. We should rise up against them. Perhaps you, too, sit there thinking that we should forget our fear and rise against those who make us afraid."

"You were at Dorkay House," one said, pointing at me. "The night some white men came to listen to the bands from Soweto."

I admitted that I had been.

"Somebody said you write books," he said. I agreed.

"Will you write about us?"

"I cannot be certain. After all I do not know your names. I will write about the conditions under which you live and perhaps, if you ever read the book, you might be able to identify yourselves." Saying it to have some real part in the conversation, not really knowing if I would write about them.

"That's good, friend. No names. Please, no names.

But if you write about conditions here we shall never be able to read your book. Not here. Don't you know that books critical of the Government are banned?"

"I know. My books *were* banned for a time."

"You heard about that Afrikaner writer, Brink? He's written a book about a White sleeping with a black woman. Hell, they're after him. The politicians, the church, everybody. Shit, everybody knows it happens. That's why they've made laws against it. But the laws don't stop people from doing what they want, it only makes them cautious. Where the hell do they think all the half-breeds, the Coloreds, come from?

"Shit, brother. Can you imagine what would happen if a Black wrote a book like that? Nobody would even publish it. Look at us. We write simply stories and songs about ourselves and nobody wants to touch them. Naturally we write about our pain and our problems, not about sleeping with some white woman. You ever heard of Benedict Vilakaizi?"

"No. Who is he?"

"He was one of the few Blacks to teach at Witwatersrand University, years ago, before this Government changed all that. He was also a poet. He wrote many poems. Go to a bookstore and ask for *Zulu Horizons.* That's the name of his book of poems. Listen to this:

> '*Yes, when a siren screeched one day,*
> *A poor black* dassie* *heard its call*
> *And, answering its summons in confusion*
> *Was trapped.*
> *And then*
> *Transformed into a mole,*
> *Was forced to burrow deep and search for*
>   *gold.*'"

*Black peasant.

"That's very good," I said.

"Shit, brother. It's more than good. It's beautiful. And it's real."

"I'd like to meet the poet," I said.

"You will, one day." Laughter. "For now, he's dead. Died about thirty years ago. But he was a real Zulu. He spoke to the heart and soul of his people, to their pain and their pride. He was a father to us, not like Buthelezi."

"What about other black writers?" I asked, wishing to keep him off Buthelezi.

"Oh, there are many. Many. But nobody wants to publish them. When a few of them get published, there's nothing much in it for them. But they, too, speak for us. Like Stanley Wotzuwadi. Listen to this:

> *'I get my cue*
> *From the glint in the cop's eye.*
> *I have seen it before.*
> *So I have to find it.*
> *I pull away from Mons and hug myself in*
> * desperation.*
> *Up, down, back, front, sides, like a*
> *Crazed tribal dancer*
> *I have to find it.*
> *Without it I'm lost.*
> *With it I'm lost, a cipher in Albert Street.*
> *I hate it. I treasure it.*
> *My pass. My everything.'*

"You understand. He's talking to me. About me. About us. No white man can understand those words."

"You know about the Book of Life? Our pass book?" one asked.

"Yes. I've seen one," I replied. "Where can I buy some books by these black writers?"

They told me of a bookshop on Commissioner Street, a few blocks away, which was known to carry books by Blacks, native and foreign.

After some further conversation they invited me to have a drink with them later and I agreed to meet them outside the railroad station a short distance from my hotel. I left them, to search for the bookshop and purchase copies of books they'd mentioned, poetry and prose by Blacks, the few who had managed to get some of their work published. As they'd directed me I took the route through Eloff Street toward Commissioner Street.

10

Half a block away from Commissioner Street I saw a black man running, just running along Eloff Street toward me, on the roadway near the sidewalk to avoid the traffic. There seemed to be no one pursuing him and I was not alerted to any trouble until two white men stepped in his way and grabbed him, one of them holding him tightly by the collar of his shirt. They were shouting at him in Afrikaans, so I could understand nothing except the repeated, "No, no, *Baas*" from him. They cuffed and kicked him, shaking him meanwhile.

A crowd quickly gathered, some of them asking what the man had done. Some of these spoke English but all I could make out was that the man had been running. The men who held him had not been chasing him, nor did they know why he'd been running. Someone called the police, who quickly arrived and took over from the two civilians, handling the man just as roughly. One policeman, a big, red-faced, crew-cut fellow slapped the man on the side of the head with a huge meaty hand, snarling at him in Afrikaans. Someone near me called out to the policeman in English to stop hitting the man. The policeman told the

[151]

bystander to shut up or he'd take him down to John Vorster Square for interfering in the due process of justice.

"Christ, is that justice?" I heard myself ask. The big policeman glared at me. I felt pitifully helpless, a stranger, unable to do anything but look on, as they dragged the man to where they'd parked their car.

The bystanders began chattering among themselves, some expressing outrage at the two who had stopped the running man, others angrily defending their action. A crazy mixture of English and Afrikaans. Whites shouting at each other. A few Blacks standing well away from it, watching but saying nothing. I was too near the center of it for comfort, dazed by the suddenness, the sheer brutality of it. I felt myself shaking and knew that I was frightened. Suddenly, unexpectedly frightened. Christ, a minute ago the black man had been running here, the slap, slap of his feet still a faint echo in my ear with the memory of his loose shirttails fluttering behind him; now, he had vanished, in the company of brutal men, probably to be beaten while screaming for mercy, no one asking questions, no one interested in explanations. If it had been nighttime, he might have been killed on the spot. For what? For being in a hurry?

At long last I realized what so many people had been trying to tell me. It finally sank in. If you're Black in South Africa, there's nothing between you and sudden violence, nothing to protect you from the hate of centuries. On the street, in your home, anywhere. Not the laws, not the courts, not the police. "Walk," they said to me, "don't run. Don't ever run." I felt exposed, brought up hard against the fact that here I could not take for granted even the simple protection of personal space that strangers in all other places respect between each other.

Slowly I walked away from there to the bookshop.

The bookshop attendant, a young, dark-haired woman, not only had the books in stock, but had read them and spoke knowledgeably and enthusiastically about them. We went downstairs to the lower floor of the shop. While I waited for the books, there would be footsteps from time to time on the stairs which were near the cashier's desk. Each time the young woman would quickly, furtively glance behind her.

It happened again and I asked, "Why are you so nervous?"

"Nervous?"

"Yes. Every time there are footsteps on those stairs you look frightened."

She blushed. "I guess you're right. It's become a sort of occupational disease. But I can't help it. Each time it happens I promise myself that the next time I'll just ignore it, but I can't."

"But why? They're only customers, like myself, coming to look and buy."

"Not always. Regularly the Security Police drop in. It's got so we can nearly recognize their feet. They come in and flip through the books on display, deciding in their own strange way what must be withdrawn, what may be sold, what jackets must be covered. It's a kind of harassment, and there's nothing we can do about it. They're always looking for Communist literature and any title that's the least bit dubious, to them, gets the book banned."

"What do you mean when you speak of covering jackets?"

"I mean just that. I'll give you an example."

With that she went to a rack and returned with a paperback copy of *The Great Gatsby*, which was published in England. The cover carried palely colored drawings of three people, two women and a man, dressed in the style of the twenties, the women's clothing little more than a frothy film over the thin pencil lines of their bodies. There was nothing even vaguely suggestive about the drawings; one could differentiate between the sexes, that was all.

"They've ordered us to place covers over these jackets," she said. "The book has recently been prescribed for Secondary Schools, and these men claim that the cover is too suggestive for exposure to the students."

I was tempted to disbelieve her but for the seriousness in her clear gray eyes.

"Jesus Christ," I said.

"Oh, yes," she replied, "They claim they are doing it in his name and in the interests of morality. Several times each week, without any advance notice, they come in, paw their way through our books and take some away, ostensibly to read and inspect them for questionable ideas and philosophies."

"Mine were banned," I said.

"Yours?" Her eyebrows raised in surprise. "Are you a writer, too? What's your name? You're not South African, are you? Your accent. Sounds English to me."

"Yes, I write. The name's Braithwaite and I'm not South African."

"Braithwaite! Of course. *To Sir, with Love.* I read in the *Mail* that you were in Jo'burg. Yes. Of course. For a while we were prevented from selling your books, even though *To Sir* was prescribed for the Training College. Can you make any sense out of that? You know they banned *Black Beauty*, the famous children's book, some years ago? That's the kind of mentality we have to deal with."

"Now I understand your nervousness. I'm sure I'd behave in the same way under similar pressures."

"Oh, in my case it's more than that. I was in jail for several years. For opposition to the Government. They jailed me under the Suppression of Communism Act, though they knew I'm no Communist. But that's a sort of catch-all. After I came out of prison I was restricted to my home for a long time. Couldn't travel or entertain friends or anything. It's like if you stopped living but went on breathing. I thought I'd get over my fear of them, but it happens in spite of myself. I suppose it's because I can't bear the thought of being imprisoned again."

Somehow her words made a far deeper impression on me than did those of the Indian who had been held in Robben Island. He was still full of pep and vinegar and, given the chance, would again be inciting resistance. But this young woman had been hurt deeply as only the insider can be hurt when visited by the wrath of his own kind.

I paid for my books and left her. At every turn the underlying ugliness in the society was breaking through the upper crust of comfort and prosperity. To keep the majority in a state of fear some of the minority must themselves become victims, spreading the virus of fear within as well as without. With my small burden of books, I walked the short distance to the railway station. The five young men were waiting for me.

"Got your books?" one asked.

"Yes." I decided to say nothing of the incident in Commissioner Street. "Where are we going for our drink?"

"Come to where we live. In Soweto."

My immediate impulse was to refuse. I'd seen enough of that place.

"I've been there. I was there today, visiting with the YWCA."

"Women!" one said, scornfully.

"We're inviting you to come and have a drink with us, brother," another said, pointedly. I realize I should have anticipated this and invited them to my hotel. They watched me, waiting.

"Okay," I said, hating myself for my weakness. What the hell was I trying to prove?

Over my objections one of them said he'd get the tickets and we walked on to the station platform. The train was there, its engine hissing impatiently, perhaps at the Blacks who were shoving and pushing each other to get on. My friends pulled me into the surging mass.

"Why do we have to get into this one?" I protested. "I can see other carriages further along."

"Those are for Whites," was the reply, by which time I was caught in the surge and propelled along into the carriage which was already packed beyond capacity. All black people, those who were lucky enough to be seated, uncomfortable under the leaning weight of the rest of us. The place stank from the limited ventilation and the crush of human bodies. I wished I'd been strong enough to refuse this invitation.

Soon I was perspiring, the cool rivulets trickling their way down my armpits and my back. My arms were pinned to my sides, the package of books a rough discomfort against my ribcage. The knowledge that the man braced against me was feeling the same discomfort helped.

"You could have been riding comfortably with the Whites," one of my friends whispered hoarsely in my ear. "For as long as you're visiting here you're regarded as White, did you know? Honorary White." He made the two words sound like a curse.

"Now you tell me," I whispered back, letting him gloat over his small imagined victory.

Through the crush, the white conductor forced his way, grabbing tickets from outstretched hands, quickly examining them, shouting at those whose tickets were not in order, abusing them, beefy, red-faced, belligerent. We swayed against his rough, onward passage. I felt helpless, with one foot barely touching the ground, dependent entirely on the pressures which kept me erect. As he elbowed his way past me, I saw the anger in his pale gray eyes, anger and contempt for the black mass through which he must claw his way.

"He's got to get the tickets before we reach Soweto," was whispered to me. "Once we got there they'd walk all over him."

With a squeal of brakes, the train shuddered to a stop. Gratefully I waited for some easing of the pressure. By twisting my head around I caught the eyes of one of my friends.

"This is a white stop," he explained. "No Blacks getting off here. We've got more than an hour of this."

Through a window I saw the legend, Braamfontein in bold lettering on the fence along the station, and beyond the red gleam of a bungalow's roof nestling under trees. Evidently a white suburb. Soon we were on our way, making more stops for the departing Whites—Langlaate, Croesus, Canada—depositing those who had been riding in cushioned ease.

I could have been riding comfortably too, as an Honorary White. Thinking of it I felt the full impact of its debasement. For all these years I'd been living proudly in my black skin, doing very satisfying things in it. In this same skin I'd spent a happy boyhood in Guyana, learning about ambition and pride and the pleasure of competitive effort from parents and teachers and others, most of them in black skins like mine—some white, but treating our black skins with respect. In this skin I'd sat with other undergraduates in an English university, pitting my intellect against theirs, confident in my abilities. In this skin I'd flown a fighter aircraft during the war, had known love, anger, despair, and success. In this same skin I'd written my books, taught Whites, and represented my country as a diplomat.

This skin had always been good enough for me. Men had admired my prowess in it. Women of many colors had found it beautiful. Never before had anyone, anywhere, attempted to change it. Yet now my color was far more important than anything I might be or do. Piss on their Honorary White! I'll ride Black.

At Canada Junction some of the crowd dismounted to find their branch lines to various parts of Soweto. We continued on to Orlando, from which we had a long walk to where they lived. We walked along a dusty, rutted road, through rough weed-grown land cluttered with stones and here and there a pile of rubble, all that remained of former homes that had been bulldozed to the ground. In the near distance the houses were little square boxes softened by the shrubs and small trees which grew around them.

At a crossroads a group of men stood in excited conversation near a car which had run off the road and now was tilted lopsidedly on the grass verge. Along both sides of the roadway people were at their doors or windows looking toward the group of men. We stopped and one of my acquaintances spoke to them in their language. There followed an outburst of sound accompanied by much arm waving.

This car and another had been involved in an accident. An argument had ensued and the police had arrived. One driver had promptly taken to his heels. The police had shouted to him to stop, and without waiting for him to comply, had shot him, there at the corner, the bloodstained grass providing mute evidence. The wounded man had been removed in the police car to hospital, but was not expected to live. A crowd had formed and the police had ordered them to disperse. The people had merely retreated to stand outside their homes, in an ugly mood, but helpless and defeated.

Who cared whether another Black was shot and killed! Perhaps, at the hospital it would be discovered that he did not have a residence permit or Book of Life, and was therefore in Soweto illegally. After all, once a black man was in the hands of the police, identity material could easily disappear. No local resident would dare complain about the actions of the police. In any case, who could they complain to? The police themselves? The white courts? No. Fear of the white man dominated their lives. Fear of sudden violence, arrest, deportation to some remote rural area.

Along the dusty street, small groups of black men and women whispered together, their voices subdued even though the police were long gone. I couldn't imagine this fearful numbness among Blacks in New York or Chicago or London or Birmingham, in Jamaica or anywhere else where large groups of Blacks lived. Perhaps, in spite of my acquaintances' optimistic talk, they were already demoralized past any resistance.

I said as much, but was told that no one trusted his neighbor enough to band together. Resisting vicious police tactics in broad daylight was one thing, but where would there be any help if the police called at night, with their guns and their dogs, carefully selecting the houses of those who'd spoken up against them? Who'd lend a hand when his neighbor was dragged out and away, no longer militant, but abjectly groveling and begging for mercy?

This they lived with, these young men, desperately trying to blow some faint sparks from their despondent spirits, willing themselves to cling to faint dreams of a freedom which grew fainter and more distant each hour. They asked me about Blacks in Harlem and the deep South of the United States, hoping to hear from me accounts of white brutality to Blacks which might offer them some small consolation in their own desperate situation. But I told them that though the American police, given the opportunity, could be just as racist and brutal, Blacks in the United States were militantly aggressive in their own defense. Somehow, these young Africans had been fed the idea that their condition was in no way different from that of American Blacks. They quoted stories of Lester Maddox of Georgia and his ax-handles and of George Wallace of Alabama defying the Court's orders, but did not know that history had already overtaken these men. They liked to tell themselves that they would one day rise up against their oppressors; they even imagined themselves engaged in covert activities against the Whites. But it was all bravado. Empty. Mere posturing.

They angered me, these young men. I thought of people I knew in Europe and the United States, black and white, who had talked with me in the fond hope that the black South African would eventually rid himself of the incubus of oppression, by the bloodiest means, if necessary. I thought of the young Blacks in my classes at New York University who'd believed that the militant projection of their blackness was a part, perhaps the most important part of their African identity. Were they identifying with this weakness, this demoralized hopelessness? These men had been bleating about the death of a brother, but in fact Tiro's death had kindled no fire, had engendered no rage. A few minutes of huddling in grief, or beating the unresponsive earth, that was all. The realities had to be faced, clamored to be faced. Tiro was dead and had already faded into the pitiful legends of yesterday. Today was now, the job in Johannesburg, the Book of Life, the quarter room in Soweto, the paralyzing fear of Whites.

As we continued on our way to the houses we passed the elementary school. From the outside it was a large solid enough structure of reddish brick built to form a hollow square, single-storied and squat, the rough mortar between the bricks suggesting haste in construction. The ground around it was red clay nearly covered by a ragged growth of weeds, kept somewhat in check by human feet, because it provided the playground area for the school. The whole was enclosed by a wire fence torn in several places.

"I went to this school years ago," one said.

"I'd like to take a look without interrupting anything," I said. "I'd like to see them without anyone putting on a show for me."

"Then just look inside. They're accustomed to people looking in. The teacher won't mind. Nobody will put on any show for you."

"How do you know?"

"I'm always poking my nose in. We need to know what's going on in the schools, so we check from time to time. Go ahead, if you like." We stopped beside a classroom. He'd said "we" as if he were speaking for some absent group or organization.

From outside the only sound we could hear was the low voice of one person, perhaps the teacher, rising and falling softly. The door was slightly ajar, and, urged by my conpanions, I opened it further and went in, followed by them.

The room was small and very overcrowded. The benches and few desks supported twice as many children as they were designed for, squashed and perched wherever they could squeeze their thin bodies. Those who missed out on the benches and desks were either standing at the back or squatting on the bare concrete floor along the sides of the room. In a room probably built to accommodate fifteen or twenty children in comfort, there were eighty or ninety. Most of them had plastic sacks in which they carried and zealously guarded their books, rulers, pencils, and other supplies.

Considering the external surroundings, the children were tidily dressed, the boys, for the most part in gray shorts and gray or white shirts, the girls in dark blue uniform dress with white bodices. They hardly noticed our entrance. Without exception their attention was raptly fixed on the teacher, absorbing his every word.

I leaned against a wall, watching what was, to me, a miracle. I'd forgotten that, in many parts of the world there still existed a ravenous hunger for learning and knowing. It had been so in my boyhood days in Guyana, even though we were never cramped like this, never oppressed in this way. But in the long intervening years of watching students and being a teacher, I'd become accustomed to other conditions, in which students needed to be inveigled, coerced, bribed, or flattered into making the smallest intellectual effort.

These youngsters were eager, their faces and eyes bright with either the enthusiasm of discovery or competition, perhaps already aware that a great deal depended on them, and knowing well that outside there were others who would gladly take their places.

The teacher nodded in our direction but continued with his lesson, apparently unperturbed by the interruption. The lesson was conducted in Afrikaans. He would ask questions and then have to select an answer from among the forest of waving hands which clamored for the chance to reply. None of the children seemed to notice the heat or the overcrowding. They were in an intensely competitive situation and were fully responsive to it. This lesson would be followed by one in English. Until the age of eight or, in some cases, ten years, the child reads, writes and does his counting in an African language, then is abruptly switched to studies conducted in Afrikaans or English or both. Blacks view this as a deliberate plan to inhibit their progress in a society which uses Afrikaans and English exclusively and interchangeably.

Obviously, there never would be any problem of discipline here, because there was no boredom. The children seemed to be soaking in every tidbit of information through eyes and ears, through their very skin. But what of tomorrow when even the minimal haven of this school would be denied them? All this youthful energy and thrust must inevitably collide with the white man's blockades and become poisoned with frustration, anger, and hate. I could almost feel it, a near tangible force, the accelerating build-up of energy as each graduating group was forced out into its own confrontation with the cold, closed world. How long would they be denied? Eventually, clubs, police dogs and even guns would not be able to subdue them, and that was exactly what the Whites feared.

Outside, my companions decided to stay in Soweto and offered to accompany me to the railway station. They seemed to have forgotten all about the drink they'd promised me. I told them I'd had enough of that and would rather suffer a taxi, if they'd help me find one.

"Can't take it more than one way?" one asked, grinning. "We make it both ways, five times a week. Anyway, you were lucky today. Nobody picked your pocket."

Involuntarily I checked. He was right.

"Would you show me where I'd find a taxi?" I asked.

"Not easy at this hour," one answered. "But don't worry, I'll run you into Jo'burg." He led the way to his home, next to which a shiny, near-new car was parked.

"I never use it for work," he said, touching it fondly.

"Can't afford to run it to the city every day. Then the cost of parking it. So I use it mainly on weekends."

"As many a late virgin will certify," another added, and all joined in the ribald laughter. Now that the matter of my transportation was settled we stood around outside his house, chatting in lighter vein with each other. Eventually, over my broad hints, the owner of the car started it up and we climbed in, the others riding only as far as their homes. On the way to the city, he was more relaxed with me, talking about his job as a warehouseman—a dead-end, but it kept him alive. In contrast to the power-cut gloom of London which I'd recently left, Johannesburg's night was lit like a fairyland, its power stations all fueled by coal. A few blocks from my hotel we stopped at a traffic light and I noticed three smartly dressed young women, black, chatting together on the pavement, their lush bodies, bright, lipsticked mouths, and bold postures seeming out of place at that hour in Johannesburg.

"If Blacks are not allowed to live in this city, where would they find clients?" I asked my companion.

"If you wait long enough you'll see," he replied. "They're waiting for Whitey. When it's dark and he thinks nobody's seeing him he leaves his wife and goes looking for black pussy."

"But what about the police? Don't they pick them up?"

"Only those who don't pay."

So much for apartheid.

"You want to hear a famous saying?" he asked me, smiling wickedly. "A real proverb? A Soweto proverb?"

"Go ahead," I said.

"The final destiny of the white man lies between the black woman's legs. Work that out, my friend."

11

Two days before I was scheduled to leave South Africa, some students from Witwatersrand University telephoned. They said they wished to visit and talk with me, and I agreed to have dinner with them at my hotel; they wanted to take me to a local restaurant, but one near-experience of that was enough for me.

I suddenly had a feeling of confusion. Talking with one of the students on the telephone had brought the old, familiar feeling of excitement which always comes to me at the prospect of meeting young people, challenging their intellects and having them challenge mine, learning from them and hoping to teach them. Life had, so far, favored me with a wide variety of experiences which lent themselves to excellent illustrations whenever I needed to enliven an academic topic. These students had invited me to meet and talk with them. They were White. For weeks now I had been bombarded by the ugliness of white bigotry toward Blacks. I'd seen a young man beaten and humiliated for no reason. He'd been running, that's all. I'd heard lovely black women talk of the fear which was a major ingredient of their daily lives. I'd traveled, cooped up with other Blacks like cattle in a truck, while Whites rode in comfort on the same train. Now here I was, reacting with pleasure to an invitation to meet and consort with Whites. Did the fact that they were students make the difference?

I wondered what the young men I had so recently visited in Soweto would think of me, if they knew I was entertaining a group of Whites. Would they consider me insensitive to their plight? But why worry about what they would think? What did I think? In the face of all the injustice I saw all around me, how could I justify to myself the feeling of pleasure at meeting the students? Perhaps, I thought, they were denied the opportunity to meet and talk with Blacks. Perhaps meeting and talking with me might sow some tiny seed of tolerance and respect which might take root. Or would it? Hell, I was not the first Black any of them had met or could meet if they wished. Or wasn't I? Maybe they'd never met another Black who'd had the opportunities to do what I had done. Perhaps, in their eyes, I was different. But, wait, wasn't that exactly what the Indian ex–Robben Island prisoner had predicted would happen? That the Whites would get to me and seduce me into believing myself different from local Blacks?

I was feeling quite low when the students arrived, but tried to hide it in welcoming them and making them comfortable. Eight of them, five men and three women, young and, at first, somewhat ill at ease. One dark-haired woman who seemed to be the leader of the group apologized for encroaching on my time, particularly as they knew from the newspapers how busy I was.

"We just had to take the chance, sir," she said. "We've read your books, we know you've lived in England, France, and the United States and we'd like to talk to you about things we'd never be able to discuss with anyone here. We just had to take the chance that you'd see us."

In the face of her plea my misgivings subsided. Hell, these young people looked no different from other groups of young Whites I'd taught in London or Denmark, New York or Florida. Perhaps, in some small way I might be useful. Wasn't this what I had always tried to do as a teacher?

We talked. At first about my books, my teaching, my travels and my diplomatic service, gradually moving on to themselves as members of their university and citizens of their country.

"All our philosophy courses teach us to examine the human condition continually and try to improve it," said one young woman, whose two thick braids emphasized the youthfulness of her serious face. "We read about social structures, historical and modern, and it is inevitable that we compare them with our own. We talk about the anomalies among ourselves. That's fine. But then we try to discuss them in class and that's where the trouble starts. How can we talk about the human condition without referring to the Blacks in our society? As soon as you mention Blacks, professors get uptight."

"Unless you refer to them only as statistics," another said.

"In High School everyone was eager to get to the university," a young man said. "We came, believing that we should develop as thoughtfully intelligent people, prepared to assume future responsibilities. And we *are* encouraged, as long as our inquiries and interests are not directed toward real social change!"

"I had this thing with my philosophy professor," one said. "We were discussing social change and after a while it struck me that our entire discussion was limited to intellectual speculation. No one had tried to draw any parallels between what we were philosophizing about and the social realities around us. No one had made any reference to Blacks; no one had commented on apartheid. Of course we talked about injustice, but not as if any of us was even tangentially involved in it. We even reviewed research that had been done, but it was as if we were discussing the behavior of caribou in Canada. So I finally spoke up and said, 'Why don't we, as students, examine our own attitudes to Blacks?' In as many words I was told to forget it."

"Why?" I asked.

"It's dangerous to display a social conscience," a young man said. "If you have a social conscience you will inevitably get around to examining Government policies and practices. So you raise a question involving the slightest criticism of that policy and the trouble starts! Some of our professors are members of the Nationalist Party and ardent defenders of Government policy. Before you know it you're under some kind of investigation."

"From your professors?"

"Worse. Much worse. From the Security Police. It's a grim situation and you find yourself spinning in circles. We study logic, so Plato's *Republic* is part of our reading. We read it and we look around to test the validity of the things we read which seem sound against the reality around us. When faced with conflicting concepts, we naturally expect to be able to talk with our professors about them. We read Mann and Thoreau and Steinbeck. French, English, German, Italian, Russian—we try to understand the views and opinions of those considered the world's foremost thinkers. Some of us have been reading Solzhenitsyn. Isn't it to be expected that we will look at our own social structure, if only to reassure ourselves that it is a good one?"

"In this society," another said, "if you entertain liberal views, you are soon forced by circumstances into testing the strength and honesty of your liberalism."

"Strength?" a young woman asked. "How can you use that word? The fact is that we assume postures. For a short while. When the pressures begin we cave in. We don't necessarily change our views but we do the treacherous thing, the humiliating thing. We cave in to the pressures applied by the university and the Security Police. We learn that there is no such thing as intellectual independence. We don't see it in our professors. We don't see it in our parents. We don't see it. Period."

"You spoke of having liberal views," I said to them. "What views?"

"That's what we wanted to talk to you about," one young man replied.Red-haired, with a full, neatly trimmed beard, he'd sat quietly since they'd arrived. "We read an interview of you in the paper the other day, and some of us have been talking about what you said. You spoke about 'social conscience.' Okay, in this society the moment the words 'social conscience' are used, we're talking about our racial situation. About Blacks. As soon as we look around to assess our social or economic situation we see Blacks. Everywhere. And we see what we do to them."

"Well, what's your attitude to them? I mean you, individually, how do you react to them?"

"I'm not sure. I try to be—"

"We're supposed to be afraid of them," the brunette interrupted him. "Everyone warns that they'll kill us in our beds one day. We're advised to be watchful of them, to keep ourselves armed always."

"Are you afraid of them?" I pointed the question directly at her.

"Not ordinarily. Not in the streets, if I see them walking. Not in the shops or offices," she stammered, then recovered. "Well, not those in our home. I mean, not when you can see them. But it's different when you think of them away from you. Where they live. What do they think? What do they talk about? My father worked many years in the Ciskei. He says they never forgive, they can go years biding their time."

"Do you think that's because they're Black? People everywhere resent injustice. If you mistreat people they are likely to turn on you. Whites do. Why should Blacks be any different?"

"It's not that they're different." From the bearded young man. "The real fact is that we don't really know them. They're all around us and we don't know them." I was glad he'd cut in. He seemed to have given the matter a great deal of thought.

"What's stopping you from knowing them?" I wanted to stir something up, get under their skins. "They're in your homes all day long. You can always begin there."

"My father said that when he was at Wits it was multiracial," a blonde girl intervened, but before she could divert him the bearded young man said, "Last summer I worked on a job with two Blacks. Okay, it was only a summer job, not much for me to do. They did all the work. One thing I had to do was sign their work permits. I suppose you've heard that a Black has to have his work permit signed by a White. Each month. Sometimes the most junior White is assigned that job. Even a girl typist might be the one to sign the permits of men old enough to be her father. I think the idea is to keep them in line, you know, humiliate them, remind them of their dependence." He licked his lips, looking around at his peers.

"Anyway," he went on, "there wasn't much to do so I'd get talking with those two. We never talked about politics and they never talked about themselves, I mean about where they lived, or their families, anything like that. We talked about sports or books or about the American and

Russian moon trips. Things like that. It was nice talking with them, they seemed to know a hell of a lot, you didn't get the feeling they were inferior or anything like that. Anyway, they got laid off, for some reason or another. I can't remember. Well, if a Black is unemployed he cannot get a monthly signature and is likely to be picked up and jailed or deported. If he goes looking for a job people always suspect the worst as the reason he was sacked. See the dilemma? Anyway, these two came to see me, met me outside one day and asked me to help them out with the signature until they could find another job. They were having a tough time, but they didn't ask for money, only the signature. Well, I knew nobody would check it, so I signed their permits. It was a funny feeling. Twenty-two years old and I held the destiny of two men at the tip of my pen. If I'd refused to sign they would have been lost. You know how it feels to have people beg you for their lives? I did it, but I never felt good or proud. Each month they'd meet me in a park and I'd sign for them. Nearly eight months. Now they've got jobs in a warehouse. I was glad when it ended, my signing, I mean. I think they even hated me a bit. They never came to tell me they'd got the new jobs; I heard it by accident. When they came for the signatures I'd sign and they'd go. No more talking together, so we never really knew each other. I don't even know what they really thought about me. Could be they hated me for having become so dependent on me. Thing is, I never felt good about helping them."

"If it's so difficult for you, it's a hundred times worse for a woman," the blonde said. "We cannot be seen talking to a black woman in a public place, let alone a black man."

"We're getting away from the point," a young man intervened, then to me.

"We're here because of the things you said in your

interview. We think you probably believe that we are either unwilling or unable to protest Government policies."

"Critical examination and challenge mean nothing in the abstract. The social, political, and economic realities all around you are crying out to be challenged," I insisted.

"You may not know it," he replied, a bit testily, "but Wits does have a reputation for criticism and protest, in spite of administration pressure and police harassment. Have you heard anything of NUSAS, the National Union of South African Students? Let me tell you. It was founded by an Afrikaner student in the old days, to encourage and support the interests of white students. It had its beginning at an Afrikaans university, and in spite of the prevailing policies of discrimination and bigotry, opened its membership to black students. That hasn't changed. If you charge that the society at large is becoming more and more polarized you may be correct, but if you looked a little closer you would soon discover that NUSAS members, black and white, are in the vanguard of action for social and political change. Many former members of NUSAS were imprisoned, sometimes in solitary confinement, for pressing for social reform. My father was one of them. I was in prep school in 1964 when the Security Police began mopping up anyone who was an activist, faculty or student. Wits. Cape Town. Rhodes and Natal. They raided all the places with NUSAS affiliation. The economics lecturer at Rhodes, Norman Bromberger, was picked up and held in solitary for a hundred and sixty-eight days. Did you know that?"

"No."

"Nowadays students are not openly activist, but they're active nonetheless. No point in getting beaten up or jailed if you can avoid it. Long before black students had formed unions, the Whites were bearing the heat of protest. Did you know that until this Government came to power there were black students at the English language universities? Did you know there were even integrated campus dances? The Government banned them in 1965. Ever heard of Sir Richard Luyt?"

"Yes. He was Governor of British Guyana just before it became independent."

"Right. He's now Principal of Cape Town U. After his appointment they resumed integrated dances there. He even offered a lectureship to a black anthropologist trained at Oxford, Archie Mafeje, but the Government forced the U. to withdraw the offer. Nearly a thousand students and faculty sat-in to protest. Dr. Mafeje was not appointed, even though the sit-in lasted nearly two weeks. Would you say that the students have been sitting on their hands?"

"No, I wouldn't." These were the things I'd been hoping to hear, not the nice, self-deprecating noises which had been made so far. But still, he was telling me of the old times. I wanted to hear about now. About here. About them.

"Meanwhile the police have become rougher in their tactics and more sophisticated in their methods. Their chief weapon was intimidation. They could easily get Afrikaner students to infiltrate student organizations. Anyone who expressed anti-Government sentiments was a target, no matter who he or she might be. Did you ever hear of Philip Golding or John Schlapobersky? They were both at Wits and were detained in 1969. A favorite police ploy was to confiscate the passport of any student or faculty member suspected of anti-Government sentiments. An American student named Rex Heinke was deported for the same reason. Don't think that all these activities were by Whites pursuing their own selfish interests."

"Weren't they?"

"No. Even after Blacks were banned from attending

white universities the white activists would meet with Blacks, surreptitiously, even in the black townships. Like everything else, the informers soon got wind of it. Some white students were arrested in Soweto, for being there without permits. That was really the year of the raids. The Security Police were everywhere, picking people up and detaining them on the flimsiest pretext. One student named Ahmed Timol died in detention it is said because of a severe beating by the police."

He seemed unable to stop himself. The stuff was flowing from him, rushing out of him, while the rest of us listened.

"Did you see in the newspaper that Abraham Tiro has been killed by a parcel bomb? They've been after him a long time. In 1972, soon after I came up to Wits, he made a graduation speech at Turfloop U., the black university in Natal. In it he attacked the racist philosophy of the Bantu Education Act. For this he was expelled. As a result all the Turfloop students staged a sit-in and all were expelled, the police helping with the expulsions. Naturally. This set off a chain reaction, as students from black universities at Fort Hare, Westville, Bellville, Zululand, everywhere, joined in spontaneous protest. The high point was a peaceful demonstration by more than ten thousand Whites on the steps of St. George's Cathedral at Cape Town. As you would expect, the police charged at them, with batons and guns, and even followed them into the Cathedral to beat them up and arrest them. Can you imagine that? Inside the Cathedral. And the Prime Minister defended them.

"I could tell you more. Do you know why? I plan to document it all; maybe I'll use it as the basis for my thesis. I was in Cape Town for that protest demonstration. I saw what happened with my own eyes. I stayed out of the way. I don't think I could take that kind of brutal beating. The police don't care whom they hit, man or woman. Or where."

"What about the black students?" I asked.

"They're harassed all the time. Even before they open their mouths they're banned. I guess the informers are even more active among them. Black informers. Every day you read of some more being banned, restricted to their own homes from dusk to dawn. However, you seem to take their protest for granted. What you wanted to know about was our involvement. If you see little evidence of it, that's because we're copying the tactics of the Blacks. We've been operating underground since 1972, when the editor and the cartoonist of the "Wits Student," our university publication, were suspended from the U. for publishing anti-government material. They were subsequently charged with offenses under the Publications and Entertainments Act and convicted. The same thing has happened at other universities, black and white. The Government has strangled protest in any overt form. I don't believe they will succeed in silencing protest. We're being forced to operate differently, that's all."

"How has the murder of Tiro affected your underground activities?" I asked. "Seems to me the Security Police have demonstrated how very easily they can reach anyone, anywhere."

"Perhaps," a young woman said, "but not necessarily. The police knew that Tiro depended on help from friends. He'd fled to Botswana, but he needed help, and the police found a way to get to him. Here we are learning to be very careful. We hadn't agreed to tell you all these things because we couldn't take the risk of your mentioning your source, if you decided to write about it."

"I won't mention names," I promised, "nor will I ask which of you are involved in what movement. But I'd like to know whether it really is a movement or just the posturings of a few?"

"We're more than a few. Much more. Even some faculty members are with us. The same is true at other universities. Unfortunately, we can't expect any public support, not even among our parents or relatives. Everybody is afraid. Even the priests. Most of them, the English-speaking ones, are sympathetic, but they can't all be martyrs. Did you know that there's a violent right-wing group operating with the knowledge and consent of the Government and Security Police? They call themselves Scorpio. They're terrorists, but because they're White there's no mention of them. In '72 they fire-bombed the home of the student president of Cape Town U., Geoff Budlender. Naturally, no arrests, no prosecutions. So, you see, we're like lambs surrounded by predators. From the distance of the U.S.A. you might imagine that this is a struggle between Blacks and Whites. It's much more than that. Under this government it's also become a struggle by some Whites for freedom to live in peace with justice for everyone, Black and White. We do not plan to turn this country over to the Blacks, but we'd prefer to see it governed democratically, justly, and without recourse to fear and intimidation."

We were interrupted by a call from the hotel lobby. Dr. Bozzoli, President of Witwatersrand University, wished to speak to me. He came on the line and reminded me that I'd promised to dine with him at his house that evening. Covering the mouthpiece, I told the students that the President of the U. was at the hotel and I thought I'd better meet him downstairs.

"On account of us?" one asked.

"Well . . ."

"I think you should ask him up," one said. The others nodded.

I asked him to come up, checked my diary and found that it was true. I'd made the entry, but on another page. I told the students of my dilemma, adding that I was sure Dr. Bozzoli had heard at the desk that I was entertaining a group of his students. The front desk seemed to know everything I did.

"They wouldn't know," I was told. "We drove into the basement garage and took the lift right up here. We knew the number of your suite from when we'd phoned earlier."

"You'll have to go with him," one said.

"I suppose so, but I was really enjoying this talk with you. And I've invited you to be my guests for dinner. What shall we do about it?"

"Whatever you say," they told me. I was unhappy to have to leave them, because we'd finally broken through the earlier resistance and were reaching each other.

"Here's my suggestion," I offered. "I'll go with Dr. Bozzoli for two hours. Meanwhile you order your meal here, whatever you like, and take your time about it. I'll be back before you're through and we can have coffee together and continue our talk."

They agreed. The President arrived and seemed quite surprised to see me with a roomful of young people. I made no attempt at individual introductions, bearing in mind some of the things we'd been discussing. They seemed a little jittery at having been discovered by him.

On the way to Dr. Bozzoli's home, I told him of my predicament and explained that the students had offered to wait for me while I kept my dinner engagement with him.

With the Bozzolis were a few members of the university community, one or two businessmen and their wives and the author Nadine Gordimer with her husband. Before dinner we sat outdoors and made small talk. For much of this pleasant interlude I listened, observing these charming, urbane, gracious people who seemed untouched and untroubled by the sinister air which foamed and rumbled about them. They talked knowledgeably about their country's economy and the implications of the extraordinary fluctuations of the gold prices. They commented on the equally dramatic changes taking place in diplomatic procedures, largely due to what they called American "instant" statesmanship as practiced by the very peripatetic American Secretary of State. They discussed the international effect of oil shortages, but assured themselves that South Africa would suffer less than most because her economy depended more on her massive coal reserves than on oil.

From where we sat, the women gowned and coiffed, the men elegant and worldly, national disaster seemed light years away. Part of me wanted only to enjoy this short respite from the hustle of six extremely busy weeks, but another part of me was watchful and listening, remembering that under the selfsame stars that glistened overhead, and within a short distance from where we sat, the pain of exclusion was being acutely felt and deeply resented by others, Blacks like myself. Within earshot of our sophisticated banalities, the fuse was already set for a tragic explosion.

Things changed when we went in to dinner. Mrs. Bozzoli, who had said so little outdoors, being content to supervise the introduction of newcomers and settle them down with drinks, now emerged as a highly articulate and well-informed hostess, displaying a surprising independence of spirit which defied compromise of her personal principles. As if under her stimulating influence, the conversation became more sober and careful, and was directed to the fundamental issues of South Africa's domestic and international situation. Inevitably, I was asked to state my impressions of the society even though I protested that I had seen very little and learned even less in the six weeks of my visit. However I said that it seemed to me the Government was deliberately trying to goad the black people to the point of revolt.

Even though their expressed attitudes vary in form, all Whites benefit from the cruel exploitation of the Blacks and are disinclined to any change likely to threaten those benefits in any way. Some of those sitting and talking with me took a distant, intellectually objective view of the racial situation, assuring me that in spite of what I might see many changes for the better were in progress. They could recall the conditions and circumstances of ten or fifteen years earlier, and were themselves impressed by the dramatic way in which changes had occurred since. They drew my attention to the recently publicized decisions to abandon some of the "petty apartheid," the segregation signs so familiar on park benches, buses, and public buildings.

Impatiently, I applauded their objectivity but insisted that I could not share it. They could afford their distance from the Blacks, because at every level that distance was maintained and encouraged. They all had black servants who were denied the right to bargain for their labor and could hardly protest their treatment. I could not be "objective." I was black and could not, would not wish to avoid identity with those of whom they spoke so impersonally, so unfeelingly. I knew that I was sitting there with them only because I was an overseas writer whose work they admired. Did they care about the authors and poets of equal or greater potential vegetating among them?

"Let's get to the heart of the matter," one woman said,

her face set in a mold of aggressive determination. "I'm a sociologist. The very nature of that discipline requires that we regularly examine our society for strengths and weaknesses. The moment we begin we're confronted with the inequities imposed on Blacks. Okay. But consider for a moment what would happen if those inequities were suddenly removed. Our elders remind us of what they endured at the hands of Blacks when this country was settled. The disparity in numbers remains, perhaps it has even increased. Just imagine the Blacks in power. Given the present conditions, what could we do to reduce what you call polarization without tipping the balance of power in favor of the Blacks?"

There was a sudden stirring among the group. Clearly, she had posed the question of general concern to them all. She caught me unprepared. I had not, so far, been thinking along those lines.

"I would prefer to speculate on the sharing of power rather than on a reversal of roles,". I said. "Think what a willing and conscientious black population could contribute to the society. Not as near-slaves but as citizens proud of their rights. In many other societies, given the opportunity, Blacks have proved themselves as capable as anyone else of setting national needs at the top of their priorities."

"It would be unreasonable not to expect them to want to revenge themselves on us for past injustices," another suggested.

"If Germany and Israel can find bases for mutual cooperation, I imagine it is quite possible for anyone else."

"In this society, the individual is expected to conform politically and socially," a bald man said. "The attitude to Blacks is both social and political. If I, as an individual, wished to adopt a humanitarian attitude to Blacks whom I meet, work with, or employ, I would automatically be assuming a posture politically at variance with the prevailing governmental policies."

"If, as an individual, in spite of the attitudes of others, you can recognize and respect the humanity of Blacks, I cannot see how that would force you into any political posture. I am Black. You can sit here and converse courteously with me; that does not suggest a political posture. You say you work with Blacks. I cannot see that, should you treat them with courtesy and respect you are assuming a political posture. If you employ Blacks as domestic servants and decide to pay them a wage you can afford and they are worth, I do not consider that a political posture, unless you wished to make it so."

"I don't think your reference to yourself is relevant," someone intervened. "You are a famous author and a stranger, so immediately our attitude to you is one of respect."

"But I am black and my presence among you should help you to appreciate the stupidity of the assumptions that Blacks are less capable, less intelligent and less human than Whites. The real difference between your black countrymen and myself lies in access to opportunity. The question you'll have to face is, how much opportunity would you wish to see granted to Blacks, the opportunity to vote, to negotiate the sale of their labor, to own land on which to build their homes, to compete according to their abilities?"

"What about the risks?" from another. "The risks of revenge on the part of the Blacks? You seem to expect us to take an objective view of what is primarily an emotional matter."

"Just as you expect me to respond objectively to your questions about Blacks," I replied.

"The point is well taken," interposed President Bozzoli. "Now, Mr. Braithwaite, in the light of what you've been saying to us, would you consider returning to spend some time here on campus? Say, three to six months as guest professor? My feeling is that it would be of tremendous benefit to this university."

Hearing the words coming from him in soft, measured tone I was immediately flattered. Then in a flash came the image of what would happen to me.

"Good God," I exclaimed.

"What's the matter?" he asked. "Have I taken you by surprise?"

"You have, but I've just realized what that would mean. Your Government could require me to live in one of the black townships. Soweto, possibly."

"What's the objection?" someone asked.

"Objection! Have you been to Soweto? No, thank you. I like the idea of living where I can afford and moving about with freedom. I won't be herded." That train ride appeared in my mind, a horrifying apparition.

"That could easily be taken care of," Mrs. Bozzoli intervened. "You could live in our house, be part of our household for the time you are here." Said so naturally, not a moment of hesitation.

"But there's the matter of movement." I was frantically searching for excuses, knocked off base by my own unpreparedness for this. Who would have imagined an invitation to stay on this White-only campus? "I'd be literally restricted to the campus. I couldn't walk into a cinema in town, or a restaurant or anything. I don't think I could stand that."

"Seems like a small sacrifice, in view of the arguments you've recently raised," some remarked. Belatedly I remembered Mrs. Bozzoli's invitation to share their home. How would I get out of that.

"I could not accept your invitation if I agreed to come back," I said to her. "It would be quite unworkable. I would need a separate place where I could meet and talk with anyone at any time without having the comings and goings imposed upon you."

"Then we'd arrange for you to have a faculty apartment." She had the reply in a moment. I felt cornered.

"Your being here would be wonderful for us, for our students and for our community," Dr. Bozzoli said. "The response you've already had should be some indication of how deeply we all appreciate what you've been saying to us. I'm sure we would be taking some small risk in having you disturb our complacency, but we are willing to take it. What about you? If we are to work together for realistic social change, it will take more than a short lecture or two. Our staff and students would need to talk with you, get a feel of your mind and spirit at close quarters. They would need to touch you, intellectually and spiritually. It would take a little time for us to learn about you and from you, as it would take a little time for you to learn about us."

"Perhaps Mr. Braithwaite's comfort is more important than his political posture," someone suggested softly, coating the barb with a light layer of laughter. I heard it and it disturbed me. Was that how they saw me?

"Dr. Bozzoli, I was completely unprepared for your invitation and would like to think about it. I must confess that my very immediate reaction to it is negative, because of how this society treats its Blacks. However, please let me have some time to think about it."

"That's very reasonable," he replied. "Sorry I sprang it on you like that, but the thought came to me just as unexpectedly. I'd like to see this university as an institution that's able to meet and accommodate a challenge. Your presence here would be very timely. If we all really want positive change to take place, some of us critics must step off the sidelines and jump into the game. I suppose I'm inviting you to take risks, but the decision must be yours. We would welcome your presence at this university."

I thought of all the Blacks who had warned me that, somehow, I would be used by the Whites. Could this invitation be regarded as a way of using me? The Principal had no doubt about my uncompromising attitude to his Government's racial policies. He was not, in any way, asking me to dilute or abandon those views. It was an invitation, pure and simple. Why should I be looking over my shoulder for those Blacks who might censure me. Hadn't I always taken pride in my personal freedom of spirit? If one of the black colleges had extended such an invitation, would I have hesitated? Was my personal comfort at issue here, as had been hinted?

I didn't know. I really needed time to think.

"Don't worry for a moment about your accommodation, or anything else," Mrs. Bozzoli insisted. "Just come, we need you."

"Very few outsiders find their way to South Africa's academic centers," a professor added. "Our students and teachers are facing the grim prospect of intellectual ingrowth. Challenge from a source uncommitted to this country could be a very important catalyst, at this time when we are all searching for answers. At least, give us an opportunity to see ourselves as we are seen, from the outside."

I wanted to shout at them, "I'll think about it!" Couldn't they imagine how depressing, how nerve-racking it was for me in their city? Would it be enough for me to be with them and the students? Was there no way in which I might, at the same time, be of service to the Blacks, for my soul's sake?

Dr. Bozzoli interrupted to explain that I had been dragged away from some students who were still waiting for me at my hotel room, thus making it easy for me to say my adieux and leave.

The students had finished their meal and were dallying over coffee and cigarettes, looking relaxed and comfortable. I wondered again what my black friends in Soweto would think of this scene if they could see it. And the young, aggressive Indian of Robben Island: wouldn't he see this as definitive evidence that I had sold out?

Before I'd left the students, there'd been some talk of underground action. I wished to learn more about that and asked them. Perhaps, in my absence they had decided they'd said enough; I made several attempts to steer the conversation back to the topics we had been discussing, but soon became aware of their resistance.

"I think we were sort of blowing off steam," one said. "When one is talking with someone like you, one is apt to overreach oneself. If you have a social conscience you cannot avoid awareness of the inequities around you. You want to do something about them, and that brings you up hard against authority. In this society authority is inflexible. So you have a choice. Either you follow the lead of your social conscience and take the risks or you shut up. If you're wealthy, you can get away with an occasional gesture, like taking some token interest in a nursery school for black children, or inviting a black writer or politician into your home. If you're not wealthy or influential, you compromise. They have ways of making you compromise, or they break you. By fear and intimidation. You know, we've been wondering something while you were away. If you were South African, how long do you think you'd last?"

"The point is," I replied, "I'm not South African. If I had been I might never have become the man I am. All the odds are against it."

For a while we continued to chat about other things, the U.'s drama program, films, sports.

Then they left. I wondered whether Dr. Bozzoli's appearance had affected them. I had introduced them collectively, so it was very unlikely that he had taken particular notice of any individual. In any case, I felt sure he was not more than pleasantly surprised to find me surrounded by a group of students, none of whom was personally known to him.

Yet it was clear that they had been turned off. For some reason fear had got into them, so there it was again. From every side I was hearing about it. Everywhere I saw evidence of it. From Blacks. From Whites. From black housewives and workers, and now from white students.

All of them, black and white, seemed powerless against the forces which intimidated and frightened them, yet there were undercurrents of rebellion; the earlier outburst of the students, the blacks' smoldering rage. With the entrenched Government resisting every effort toward positive change, the future offered nothing but violence and bloodshed. The Government was ready for a confrontation. Their huge stockpiles of armaments and their aggressive intransigence suggested that they would even welcome it. Everything pointed to a collision course.

12

The following day was spent in preparation for my departure from South Africa. The officials at the Tourist Bureau who advised me were courteous and helpful, clearly concerned with projecting the right image. While waiting there, I picked up a copy of the day's *Rand Daily Mail*. It carried a story on the Government's intention to impose new curbs on "some groups." The State President, Mr. Fouche, warned that a number of pressure groups were "trying to bring about unconstitutional political, social, and economic change in South Africa," and claimed that "implicit in their call for change was the threat of internal violence. These groups do not have in mind normal evolutionary change," Mr. Fouche was quoted as saying. "They are bent upon radical, even revolutionary political activities." He claimed that they were financed from abroad and expressed the Government's determination to curb them. Oblique reference was made to NUSAS and the black South African Students' Organization, most of whose leaders were already banned or restricted.

In the opposition's response to Mr. Fouche, Mrs. Helen Suzman, the most vocal, spoke in defense of the predominantly white NUSAS, saying, "I do not always agree with everything NUSAS does, but I hope there are enough who will see that the Government does not financially starve NUSAS into submission. I believe it is important that NUSAS be allowed to operate. This is an organization of young people who care about racial injustices . . ."

Not a single word in defense of SASO, the black organization.

A shocking story caught my attention. An eleven-year-old black child, Godfrey Lambert, had been picking up pieces of coal at the Beaufort West railway yard and was caught by three white railway workers who undressed him, smeared his body with grease and held him in front of the fire door of a blazing locomotive engine. The child had been literally roasted and was horribly scarred, physically and psychologically.

"At night he wakes up screaming," his mother said, adding that she feared her son's mind was permanently damaged.

The white railway workers were each sentenced to six lashes and a year's imprisonment, suspended for three years.

I tried to imagine a parallel situation in which three Blacks brutalized a white child. In a South African court, the death penalty would have seemed lenient punishment indeed!

God, could I in my right mind consider returning to this country to work and live among people who could condone such atrocities? To suspend sentence on three such savages was nothing short of condoning their act. Reading about it stirred the rage inside me. In fact, reading the newspaper altogether was a frustrating exercise. The entertainment page advertised theatre, cinema, concerts, dogracing, etc., but I knew those ads were not directed to me and other Blacks. No need to include the "Whites Only" tag. But why the hell was I even bothering to think about it? Had I indeed been seduced into imagining myself exempt? Christ! Chasing around the country as a tourist with hardly a moment to spare was one thing. Wherever I went the Information Office would get the word there ahead of me and dictate that courtesy be shown me. Living in Johannesburg for three months within sight and sound of familiar amenities would be quite another thing.

Could I cope with it? What did it matter if my color barred me from cinemas and restaurants and bars? Was my own comfort so overriding a priority? The native Blacks had each known a lifetime of exclusion from all these things. Wouldn't the work with students and faculty be enough? I could always seek out my fellow Blacks in the black townships. If my feeling of identification was real, why did that prospect bother me?

And that other thing, the continued probing and questioning from the Blacks themselves. How much more of that could I take? Their sly, oblique quizzing always made me feel guilty of the comfort I enjoyed, the privileges I could exercise. But had I not earned each privilege, each area of comfort? Was I not autonomous, free to design my own life, answerable only to myself? Outside South Africa any of these Blacks could live as I live, be free to fulfill himself. Why should I be on the defensive? Why should I allow myself to be forced into playing someone else's role?

If I returned to South Africa, Dr. Bozzoli promised complete access to students and faculty, and complete freedom to be myself, thinking as I thought, believing as I believed, making no secret of my distaste for their racial policies. How long would they and the Government accommodate me and my views? Dr. Bozzoli probably thought he was making me a simple proposition. Hell, about as simple as the maze of a man's life.

Early next morning I packed my bags. All that remained was to pay my bill and get out to the airport. In the park across the street the scrawny black boys were already at their interminable games, dodging between the black workers who hurried past them. Hungry, uncared-for, this was their youth. What of their tomorrow and adulthood? Did they have any hopes, any aspirations? Did they know anything about love of country, these children who had been denied even love of family? It is said that the future of a country is invested in its youth. What part of South Africa's future was invested in these boys?

The hotel receptionist had proudly mentioned the national motto, "Unity is Strength." Where was the unity? Was the strength that of arms and armaments? Was it understood that the words completely excluded any participation by Blacks? From my window the view offered a sense of ordered progress, of controlled growth, with no sign of the suppurating evils and the frustration and hatred they bred.

Those hurrying black figures seemed concerned only with getting to their jobs on time, neatly dressed, faces revealing nothing of their thoughts. Where did I hear that the black man was content with his lot? Those hurrying men and women were no different from myself except in experience of living in freedom.

At the hotel entrance, the car was waiting to take me to the airport.

About the Author

E. R. Braithwaite is a graduate of Cambridge University and has an M.A. in physics. He has been an RAF fighter pilot, a teacher, a lecturer, and a children's officer for the London Welfare Department. In 1965 he was named the Head of Mission for Guyana at the United Nations. He has additionally been appointed Guyana's Ambassador to Venezuela, Human Rights Officer for the World Veterans Federation in Paris, and Education Consultant for UNESCO in Paris. Most recently, Mr. Braithwaite was Writer in Residence at Florida State University.

Mr. Braithwaite's earlier works include *Paid Servant*, *A Kind of Homecoming*, *Choice of Straws*, and *Reluctant Neighbors*. *To Sir, with Love* was published in several languages, drew wide critical and public acclaim, and became the popular movie of the same title.